BALLOONING

With fond memories of Jo and Nini Boesman,
Jacques Demenint and Albert van den Bemden,
who all initiated me into the extraordinary,
beautiful and exhilarating pastime of
ballooning.

Anthony Smith

BALLOONING

Anthony Smith and Mark Wagner

Patrick Stephens Limited

An imprint of Haynes Publishing

Acknowledgements

Anthony Smith would like to thank those several dozen members of the British Balloon and Airship Club who gave so generously of their time in helping with the preparation of this book. There can be no better reason for founding a club than making happy and extensive use of all its expertise, when need be, very much later on.

Mark Wagner, relatively new to the ways of ballooning, is grateful to those who went out of their way to allow photographic access, flights and those who offered to disembark at the last minute due to excessive amounts of camera equipment preventing balloons from lifting off. In particular – Colin, Tessa, Lucius, Clare, Sara and Helen, at Flying Pictures, Richard Mold, Robin Batchelor, Chris Dunkley, Piers Glydon, Chris Perrett, Greg Miller, Steve and Jed Davis, Bob McGee, Nick Calvert, Jim and Mike Howard, Paul Dolby, Chris Aindow, Steve Maynard, Terry Duffell, Karen and Neil Gabriel, Peter Bish, Rob Bayly, Brett E. Schuler, Capt. Ian Johnson, Paul and Chris Gingell, Steve Byles, Austin Brown and Allan Winn.

Photographic credits:

Thanks are due to the following for photographs supplied:

Rob Bayly: PP 172, 174, 183 (L).

Peter Bish: PP 18, 68, 82, 85, 87, 88, 92 'Golli' and 'FT', 94, 102, 114, 140, 150, 153, 154, 156, 158, 180.

Flying Pictures: PP 121, 122, 123, 124, 125, 126.

Karen and Neil Gabriel: P 106.

Joe Hanson: Front cover.

Peter Nicholson: P 98 (2).

Raven Industries Inc: PP 53.

Rex Features Ltd: PP 183 (R).

Anthony Smith: PP 171, 173 179,182.

First published in 1998

British Library Cataloguing-in-Publication Data:

A catalogue record for this book is available from the British Library

ISBN 1 85260 568 5

Library of Congress catalog card no. 98-71567

Patrick Stephens Limited is an imprint of Haynes Publishing, Sparkford, Nr Yeovil, Somerset BA22 7JJ
Telephone: +44 1963 440635 Fax: +44 1963 440001 E-mail: sales@haynes-manuals.co.uk Web site: http://www.haynes.com

Haynes North America, Inc,. 861 Lawrence Drive, Newbury Park, California 91320 USA

Designed and Typeset by Camway Autographics, Sparkford, Nr Yeovil, Somerset BA22 7JQ

Printed in England by J H Haynes & Co. Ltd.

Foreword

Ballooning occupies a special niche in the field of aviation. Whereas most other forms of flight began with a shaky foothold, developing into complex and expensive technological wonders, ballooning for the most part retained its romantic image of being the least expensive but most enjoyable way to achieve flight. Surprisingly, ballooning was, for over 120 years, man's only means of conquering the skies. Once the heavier-than-air machines matured, however, ballooning continued mainly as a gentleman's pursuit.

With the advent of nylon fabric and propane burners in the late sixties, we suddenly had hot air ballooning within the reach of everyone – it became a hobby, it became a sport and it became a business for many balloonists.

The sight of a balloon is a happy one. It is a harmless and proud machine; a gentle giant that will bring smiles to faces and always entertain. It is colourful – more so than any other aerial vehicle, as you are about to experience.

Whilst there will never be a substitute for the real thing, this book goes further than any other towards bringing ballooning to your doorstep. Anthony Smith's literary genius has kept us entertained for more years than I can remember, and he remains unchallenged as the finest lighter-than-air correspondent. His writing style is highly unusual, poetic, amusing and informative all at the same time.

Last but not least, ballooning is visual and Mark Wagner's stunning photography is incredibly colourful and dramatic, and the best we have seen so far.

Per Lindstrand

CONTENTS

CONTENTS

It was the earliest form of aviation and, say some, still the best, however different the modern means to rise and join the sky.

CHAPTER 1

Setting the scene

Who else starts a journey without knowing where it will finish? And who stands on wickerwork to get there, wherever it is? Who is driven by the wind without feeling a puff of its exuberance, and who else lands without brakes of any kind, before falling over, laughing, and then – the greatest strangeness of all – is delighted and eager to do it again?

CONDEMNED PRISONERS were suggested as the earliest aeronauts, until brushed aside by two aristocrats who made the prime ascent. One of these would soon die, becoming the first aviation casualty 19 months later, but there was never shortage of applicants to fill his place. And there has never been shortage in all the years since then. Balloons still go where they please. They still have baskets and no brakes, and their travellers still land, either upside-down or right end up, as they have always done, but there are today more balloons and balloonists than there have ever been in the 215 years of ballooning history.

The sport of ballooning is currently the fastest growing form of aviation. In Britain hardly a field has escaped the sudden arrival of a basket for the event which balloonists call a landing. Mere observers, assuming a certain absence of control, call it mayhem. They are astonished that anyone, let alone all involved, survive such dishevelment. And then laugh before packing up the contrivance that so nearly laid them low as it descended from gentle heaven to reach the solid ground. It is not an aircraft using wheels upon a purpose-built runway – far from it, but is the very first thing that flew. And, say some, nothing better has since been fashioned for voyaging through the air. It permits a form of flying like none other. It is extraordinary and supreme.

A balloon looks so very right when floating in the sky. It is not a harsh invader, as is an aeroplane or, worse still, a helicopter. It looks as if belonging there, as clouds do, as thistledown, as every other floating thing. Contrarily a balloon can look so very wrong when reaching a take-off site, all bundled within a car or no less compressed inside a trailer. Its basket is a basket, that is all. The envelope is compact within its carrying bag, a canvas sack with handles. Other related bits and pieces seem no more portions of a flying machine than do an attic's contents or the objects which, given half a chance (or less), spew forth from unkempt cupboards.

'Got everything this time?' ask passing friends (forever fusing mockery with conviviality).

There is cause for such enquiry. Hot air balloonists should not (but can) forget the burner, its various hoses, the propane cylinders, the straps for holding them in place, the crown line, the internal lines, the fan, the basket poles, the instruments,

...A balloon does look so very right when floating in the sky. It is not a harsh invader, as is an aeroplane or, worse still, a helicopter. It looks as if belonging there, as clouds do, as thistledown, as every other floating thing...

…The people, the inmates of that dragging thing, then realise they are undamaged, but often disarrayed. Or not quite the right way up, whichever way that ought to be…

and maps, and perhaps a radio, and some food, and drink, and telephone numbers (almost certainly), and – oh, yes – matches or a lighter to ignite the flame. The assortment for gas balloonists smacks even less of aviation: 80 small sacks (at least), a wooden hoop with toggles, 200 feet of thick rope, other lesser ropes coloured red and blue, 9,000 square feet of envelope (or more) and a wide-meshed net big enough to entrap a whale. Attics and overladen cupboards could be envious of such diversity.

'Got everything?' ask further passers-by, self-giggling at such ancient wit.

In truth the balloonist is also curious at the assembly. Is this really the wherewithal for flight? More to the point, is it all in good condition? Will each piece fulfil its proper role without snapping, bending, rending at, say, 500 feet? Many a motorist, observing a vehicle's bowels when these are jacked high within a garage, is amazed that lives are ever entrusted to all that iron and tube and pipe. For balloonists the bowels are exposed at the outset. They are handled, pulled, stretched, and tested gingerly for strength and worthiness. Things can seem strong enough when on the ground, but 500 feet is high enough to kill. So is 20 feet… if something does break, or tear, or yield… and should the fates decide.

That does not stop ground-based jollity.

'All present and correct?'

'Yup. All correct for the present.'

'Expecting trouble then?'

'Only if you keep standing on that rope.'

'Rope! Is that what it's supposed to be?'

Perhaps all banter is childish, inbred, pointless and fun, but every now and then it is halted when altitude is remembered once again. 'It doesn't matter what you do', as the Air Force instructed us, 'so long as you don't hit the ground when doing it.' The ground does kill, but so can other items, such as fire. A leaking propane pipe can lead to flame very speedily, particularly when a huge burner is alight nearby. Awesome pylon wires hanging in the sky do pack a terrible punch, but even lesser and straighter varieties, leading to farms and houses, can melt basket rigging to send a basket's occupants headlong to the ground.

'Got enough propane?' say the same old passers-by, like knee-jerk conversationalists telling you it is a fine day or looks like rain.

Inflating a balloon is merriment, laughter and joy, with only occasional (justified) twinges of anxiety trying to spoil the show. The sad sack of envelope material is first straightened, then spread out, then fanned with air and finally subjected to blasts from the burner. Its shape writhes as cold air gives it form, and

Almost anywhere will serve

then tautens when warmer air arrives to give it life. Helpers pulling on its crown line keep the growing form horizontal as long as possible, and yield only when buoyancy demands (and gets) the upper hand. The fabric rises eagerly, as if aware a flight is near, like dogs too excited much too soon when a walk seems imminent. The balloon's burner, after being fired parallel to the ground, now flames upwards as the basket assumes its proper place, as wires tighten, and as the whole device, from being weighty items on the ground, becomes light-heartedly ready to ascend. Those in charge give intermittent shouts above the burner's roar.

'Get in, you and you.' 'No, over there.' 'Pick that up.' 'Here, lift this.'

And then perhaps some silence, with the balloon tip-toeing on the ground, its eagerness apparent and its lift almost matching the weight of everything. Is that everything as it should be? What about the air-filled chamber up above, and its several ropes which should be pulled to check their functioning? The pilot looks past, round, and over the others on board, says different things to different people, remembers the car-keys in his pocket, and then considers all is set to go.

'Right, let's flee,' says one pilot in particular.

Further squirts of flame tip the balance from inadequate lift to just enough, and soon the whole assembly – basket, cylinders, envelope, burner, waving passengers – ascends into the air. It is magic all over again. However many times this has been done – achieved by those on board and observed from down below – it is forever special. Perhaps midwives feel the same with every birth, or ship-builders at each launch. The balloon had been earth-bound, as is the rule for every solid thing, but then is airborne. It no longer sits or slumps, but floats. It also moves, being immediately welcomed by the air as brand-new companion, as a multi-coloured extra for all the atmosphere. First-time passengers tend not to speak initially, being so absorbed in excess of novelty. Or they may exclaim, meaninglessly, using noises more than proper words, while admiring or trembling at the changing scene on every side. And it *is* on every side. There are 360 degrees of amazement, the receding take-off place, the advancing landscape, the astonishments in each direction.

There is also what has been called the Root effect (named for the man discovering this truth when suspended over Africa). At ground level a basket's sides present major problems for every would-be occupant. Like horses confronted by a hedge beyond their powers, and then landing spread-eagled on its summit, many passengers-to-be become all thighs and awkwardness when encountering a basket's rim. Kind hands lend assistance, tugging at limbs and unsheathed flesh, until upright decorum is restored. After take-off that same basket rim becomes a convenient elbow-perch, much like the counter of a favoured watering-hole; but at 10,000 feet it is again transformed. The basket's height has shrunk, many of us will swear (as Root himself did swear), to a fraction of its former size. It has become no more than an edge marking a precipice. It is certainly not, and never could have been, an obstacle to be overcome with difficulty, as pieces of oneself are left behind during the effort to climb on board. From Beecher's Brook to modest rim is very marked indeed.

So too the transformation of the land. It had been familiar, with people near at hand, with trees standing tall, with horizons obscured by objects in between. As the balloon rises the land below becomes a map, a two-dimensional thing. Its roads can be seen in their entirety, and why they travel as they do, skirting that lake, missing that major home, and leading indirectly from village A to village B, much as some casual walker might at first have strolled along that trail. Also no two fields (at least in Britain) are ever identical, in shape, in colour, or their patterning.

'Look at what I call their treble clefs,' an airborne farmer once exclaimed. 'You've always got some seed left after you've sown a field. So what do you do with it? Well, you just go back in the field, forget about being regular, and drive anywhere until it's all gone. Look, there's a good one there.'

I looked, and there was a wiggly track, a mark I had never seen, but have seen since then, over and over again.

'That's bronze age, for sure,' said an archeologist friend, the shape below being round, rather than rectangular as in later history.

It is so easy to see these patterns detailing earlier existences. Then comes realisation that the land has been used throughout the centuries by successive waves of people. The place below may now be sewage works or 'supermart', a stately home or far less stately in-fill site, but Normans tramped that way. So too

The sad sack of envelope material is first straightened, then spread out, then fanned with air and finally subjected to blasts from the burner.

Saxons and Angles, Romans and their opponents, plus all manner of earlier people who lived and died on the self-same earth after retreating ice permitted them to do so. It is a naive thought that others have existed at other times on all the land beneath, but a balloon encourages such gentle cogitation better than every other kind of aerial device.

It also permits voyeurism of a novel form. Who would have thought, save those whose lust and cunning gave rise to the idea, that cornfields are ideal for supreme intimacy? Fifty yards within those stems there exists a secrecy which cannot more readily be gained (save in well-locked rooms). As bonus the air of countryside is often warm and sultry. The sky can be a perfect blue. And the corn itself will soften solid ground, as well as shielding intimate proceedings from every prying eye. Save, of course, when a balloon flies overhead, its ring-side occupants abruptly aware of a spectacle below. And who then, owing to the wind, are firmly (and quite correctly) moved away, making them wonder what further sights there might have been had there been further time to stare.

The silence of a gas balloon, spared the noisy bursts of hot-air flame, can emphasise how very horizontally we live our lives. Shout from above at terrestrial humans, be they riding a bike, rowing a boat or merely idling, and not one of them will look upwards for the source of whatever statement came their way. The naked girl sunbathing in her garden first sat up, but only stared at the garden's walls when comment reached her ears. Realising, as she did (and so did we), that their brickwork was sufficiently high to forbid inspection she soon relaxed again. We, emboldened in our childishness, identified her more precisely, remarking on the discarded polka-dots lying by her side. Her next sitting up was speedier, and her anxiety plainly greater, but she never glanced skywards where one colossal thing, suspending a basket of smothered laughter, was drifting gently by. We, for our part, were as quiet as mice, and also a touch ashamed.

I should add, hastily, that most flights are on a nobler key. Wind blowing across long grass creates beauty of heart-thumping joy. A single deer, prancing with delicacy, can be enchanting. So too fish heading determinedly upstream, or a skein of geese far below. Even villages can seem so very right,

Drifting within the sky above Bowood, Wiltshire. There seems to be no shape which the makers of balloons cannot recreate – whether cars, houses, flowers or whatever – but all have a basket, a burner and a pilot somewhere down below.

with their solemn churches and ancient oaks, their pubs, their schools, their ponds and pathways, people and dogs, and all their cats dozing out of sight from normal eyes. There is a logic, less conspicuous when seen, as is usually the case, from somewhere on the ground. Of course, when seen from up above, the road will bend that way, with church, stream and hillock forcing it to do so. And how right that the aged pub is precisely where it is, midway between other kinds of need, the ancient smithy, the barn, that row of homes, the raw material of past lives.

Scale also becomes more correct when observed from such a slow-moving and aerial vantage point as a balloon. Maps, save those almost as big as the land they represent, do distort. Road maps in particular, with their network of arteries, imply that almost all ground has been paved for the motorists' delight. This is quite untrue. To hold a 1:50,000 map, the large scale variety (and modern variant of the 1 inch to 1 mile), while also looking at the land it portrays is to see the fallacy. The map's roads, churches, streams, canals, railways and farm-steads are far larger than their actual counterparts. Such items must be drawn relatively bigger than life to be clear. All the map's roads, save for the very widest and the most minute, have a width of almost 1 millimetre (on the 1:50,000 scale). If they were truly that size there would be space enough for 20 cars. If little streams were as big as the map's blue lines they would be major rivers, rather than slivers of water across which boys can jump. With churches, homes, schools, roads, rivers and canals *all* drawn larger than is the case any village equipped with each such item will be far greater on the map than in life. Certain individuals, like planners, environmentalists, surveyors, conservationists, should be forced to fly by balloon from time to time to see truth, and the proper scale of things, instead of burying their heads forever in the caricatures of maps.

But what is this about forcing anyone to fly in a balloon? The terrific experience should never need coercion. At its most basic it means leaning on a padded wicker rim (before the Root effect has taken hold) while watching the world go by. There is no trudging, up hill, down dale, because the hills, dales and every form of ground are passing quietly by. So do all ground-based features, that wall, that privacy, that factory and that army camp. A balloonist travels without the need even for lifting feet.

...Balloon rides are not country walks and, however many times they have been done, there is awareness (or should be) that travel by basket is more chancy – at any altitude – than standing on the ground... Chateau d'Oex, Switzerland.

Therefore 100 per cent of attention can be paid to the sights being unfolded, as if from some moving scroll, below the basket's rim. There is a tendency to look forwards, but every other way will serve as well. It is good to look back, or straight down upon an earlier enchantment, and use changing angles for yet greater satisfaction. It is not all-round vision as from some hill-top, but an altering all-roundness, a steady stream of astonishments, a perpetual feast as to what might happen next.

As extras there are all the smells and sounds to add to every sight. 'Ah, pigs!' says someone, before looking for the source. And why is that dog, busily exclaiming in the only way it can, so obsessed with our existence? Ordinary vehicles, such as trains, planes or cars, deny their passengers every form of yapping, neighing, mooing, grunting, yelling, snorting, bleating that is part and parcel of the scene, just as they withhold all the scents and odours, the fragrancies and pungencies which are wedded to the sights. Blind people can (and do) like to float above the land, knowing when ripe corn must be beneath, or woodland silently dark and dank save for squawks of protest from pheasants far below. We humans thrive on our senses. Ballooning humans welcome information from every one of them more markedly than when based upon the ground.

Perhaps fear has sharpened appetite. Balloon rides are not country walks and, however many times they have been done, there is awareness (or should be) that travel by basket is more chancy – at any altitude – than standing on the ground. A trip, or stumble, when down below is soon forgotten. A malfunction up above can be prelude to disaster. Clunks (or a sudden silence) from a motorcar will have its driver halting as soon as possible, but no such immediate solution exists for a balloon. There is the landing to be achieved, either precipitately (with the balloon in charge) or more graciously (with the pilot effecting some control). Of course there is anxiety. It is most reasonable.

'Are you afraid?' I once asked a passenger when we were standing on wicker a mile above the earth, zapping along at 40 miles an hour, and watching one black cloud promising all manner of changes in the weather.

'No,' she replied, 'should I be?'

She then sat upon the basket's edge, relaxed still further and gazed more vertically at the ground. Another passenger, on another day, chose to sit upon the basket's floor the moment we reached tree-top height. There he stayed for the remainder of the day, experiencing nothing and seeing nothing, save (one presumes) for conflagration, dismemberment, maiming and death conjured within his head. We all possess skull operators, ever willing to click on one-reelers outlining what might occur should ill-fortune come our way. Although frightened passengers can be disarming I prefer them to other kinds who stand (ye gods!) upon the basket's rim before waving, with arm and leg, at the world in general. And then pretend to slip. And then slip without pretence before doing it all again. I would sigh with relief if misjudgement got the upper hand, making them plummet from my view.

Most people, of course, are intermediate. They look over the edge (rather than stand on, or shiver behind it). They have probably worried about vertigo beforehand, and are then amazed that such apprehension does not dominate. Individuals who weaken at the knees when contemplating cliffs, and who consider four ladder rungs to be quite sufficient, are delighted that a balloon's altitude is of little consequence. Human eyes

need a tapering, a connection between ground and sky, to make mere height correctly frightening.

I learned this truth when flying on a cloudless day in the gentlest of breezes before encountering a near-vertical column of smoke from cement works a thousand feet below. Our group had been discussing whether that smoke would be gritty, foul-smelling, hot, or all three, when suddenly, after flying into it, we four shrank from the basket's edge as if repelled. Neither heat, stench nor taste of effluent had affected us; it was the sense of contact with the ground. We had all looked down that plume of smoke, and the sight had been unnerving. It had become a sudden cliff before our eyes, the longest ladder ever seen. This

Below: For once the retrieval crew are on hand as their balloon comes in to land.
Right: However many times it has been done, the take-off is always magic all over again.

fear vanished – mere seconds later – when we had left its cause. The smoke, safely behind us, then let us mock our nervousness, enabling us – once more – to enjoy the day and wonder at the sights.

Birds, as ever, flew well below for they travel no higher than need be. Indeed there is good reason for them to flit amongst the trees if aerial predators are around (and these, presumably, should always be assumed). Deer ran along the lines of corn, and the rows of planted trees. Of course they would, and do, with such truths learned more readily from a balloon. Church roofs have moss more on one side than the other. Winds blow sinuously across fields, with wheat or barley, grass or maize leaning in waves to its caress. Hares lollop, as if uncertain where to go. Rabbits run fast, only to stop abruptly (with holes nearby). Everything, or so it would seem, is arranged and displayed for the delight of those who stand and stare from their moving platform up on high.

These watchers and starers are not averse to having humans stop and stare at them. Indeed aerial travellers can take modest umbrage when some tedious pedestrian fails to respond after cat-calls and whoops of joy are shouted from above. Is he not enchanted that a balloon, a beautiful thing of colourful excitement, is doing him the honour of passing overhead? Is he so dull of soul that a tilting of his neck, the better to witness a basketful of rapture, still lies beyond him? Let us therefore shout yet louder to snap him into line. Or could it be – dread thought – that he was happy brushing through the grass, sniffing the morning air, listening to the trills of birds, and did not relish the intrusion of 100,000 cubic feet of heated air with all its ribaldry.

There is assuredly some 'Look at me!' about ballooning. These words, spoken so early in every infant life, perhaps remain more fundamental than we admit. They can certainly surface, shamelessly, among individuals floating through the air.

'Hey you, riding that bike, take care you don't fall. Yes, we're right above you. Look up and you'll see us. Oh, look out, you're going to fall! You *are* falling! Whoops! I bet that hurt. Terribly sorry.' And the balloon overhead goes merrily on its way, its occupants firing quip after quip until some further target comes in view. It has been known for shot-guns to be fired upwards. Aeronauts are first shocked and then astounded that this should

Middle left: A Russian Doll balloon – from the inside.

Left: The complete flying machine – for that is what it is – never looks much when arriving at the take-off spot.

Top left: Nor does it look much when deflated at the landing site.

Right: The faster the touch-down, the greater the dishevelment for those on board.

ever happen. 'How can anyone not be delighted when a balloon has come their way?' Grandiloquence can even increase should the inferiors down below choose to take note of, or actually speak to, those who are up above. 'It's made of nylon,' shouts one pilot to each and every query coming from the ground. 'Wo are vee, und iss ziss Engeland?' is basket talk amusing only to those on board. Every ground-based activity provides fuel for such devastating wit. 'NO BALL!' is shouted as the bowler delivers, causing consternation. 'HARD A'PORT K5', loud-hailed to the yacht in question, will create quadrupled joy if K5's helm is then sharply turned to ram K2. Juvenile delinquency, it would seem, is not the prerogative solely of juveniles.

Flying at major altitude inevitably leads to an entirely different mood among each basket load. Gone are earth-bound humans, now too small for mockery. Gone are earth-based noises, the roar of every motorway, the canine yapping, the snarl of solitary cars eating up their miles. Smells have also disappeared. Instead a better sense of landscape has arisen, an awareness of the country as a whole. There may be clouds down there, helping with comprehension of our earthly atmosphere. When a balloon is travelling at, say, 20 miles an hour this means the entire mass of surrounding air is also going at that speed, the tons and tons of it serving as blanket for our world. Go higher still, perhaps to

15,000 feet, and the thinning of that air becomes easier to understand. Any exertion leads to faster breathing, and stupid mistakes are simpler to achieve, very much simpler. At 20,000 feet it is wise to have extra oxygen although (in my experience) there is not a sense of deprivation. There is only accumulation of error (which may not be recognised until descending once again).

Sometimes, at altitude, the entire earth can vanish from view. Clouds may form, utterly silently and often speedily, to sever all contact with down below. The experience is both intimidating and exciting. There is nothing to be seen, a strange occurrence in itself, as normally we are so beset with imagery. The balloon and one's companions are clear enough, close at hand, but – beyond them – absolutely nil. Mariners may feel the same when alone at sea, but the water is on every hand, varying its complexion and squirming busily. Balloonists, suspended within air and with vision curtailed by the whiteness of cloud, can seem more utterly alone. This is even truer should the flight be solitary, away from other people, away – as near as feasible this side of

missions to the moon – from everything.

Forever providing an edge to all forms of aerial endeavour lies the fact that landings have to be contrived. With balloons these are more irregular than with other forms of aviation, their flight endings being a happy compromise between destiny and choice. A touchdown is often the most memorable portion of an entire flight, and certainly most likely to cause hurt. It leads to the majority of stories, when the day's events are being recalled, and for passengers and first-timers it is undoubtedly – after concern about vertigo – the major anxiety.

Pilots, in general, like landings best when observed by the ground-based retrieval team. Such observation is harder after touch-down, and it is good to see – and be seen by – occupants of the retrieve vehicle before descending out of sight. Their earthly task involves far more than a blind following of the balloon. Great skill, anticipation, and often speed, are necessary. The craft they are pursuing makes light work equally of railway lines, canals, hills or towns. It sails blithely over each and every one without regard to their varying effect upon the roads. The retrieval crew, only able to journey upon tarmac (save for a few exceptional circumstances), must suddenly make detours and evasions before hurtling along the straightest courses to keep pace with the balloon's leisurely haste of, say, 15 miles an hour. It is not good to follow too precisely, to take minor roads leading to farm tracks leading – probably – to nothing whatsoever. It is better to appreciate that the balloon is flying, more or less, in a straight line, to draw that line upon a map, and make wise use of larger roads until landing time arrives.

Best of all is to read the pilot's mind, to know his fuel consumption, and assess when he might be pondering a return to earth. Balloons are not landed wholly arbitrarily. Good fields are those without a crop, without livestock, without electricity, and with easy access. Retrieval teams know these basic rules and, if clever – if stupendously clever, can get ahead of the balloon and even be waiting in the landing field *before* the balloon arrives. Everyone concerned, whether ground crew or air crew, farmer or mere onlooker, is then astonished by such foresight, such mastery of the retrieval art, such brilliance. I

Facing page: Sometimes, at altitude, the entire earth can vanish from view, but somewhere down there is Leeds Castle set in the countryside of Kent.

Left: At ground level, normal life can become totally deranged when balloons are dropping from the sky, almost like apples as and when they choose.

know the feeling vividly, having achieved it – just once.

Most landings are nothing like so well contrived. The pilot descends to 500 feet or so in preparation. A field ahead looks perfect. That field is then jettisoned, so to speak, when unexpected wind makes it impossible. Another field then looms. And then perhaps another, save that each newcomer is (usually) nothing like so satisfactory as its predecessor. There is electricity at the start of the field finally selected, and some kind of barn at its other end. Its ground surface then changes from a lavish green, as seen from higher up, to a flint-rich, rocky unevenness, casually dotted with blades of grass.

'Oh well, it will have to do.'

People do not step out of cars at 20 or 30 miles an hour. Nor are they usually contained within a basket, but balloonists are (often) landing at that sort of speed and (always) within that kind of container. Passengers – and pilots – can go quite quiet at this moment in their lives.

They do have cause. Will they miss that electricity? If so will they be able to descend sufficiently speedily after passing it – but please not too speedily – to hit the ground and actually stop before arriving at that barn? The ground accelerates as it approaches, or rather as it is approached. The barn gathers speed towards the balloon – it always seems that way. Surely, so sense all first-timers (and often others longer in the tooth), everything – ground, barn, basket – is travelling much too fast. A crash is inevitable, and the skull operator swings into action, showing scenes of collision, fracture, unconsciousness, mayhem, death. Surely it will…? Surely it…! Surely…!

Then the basket hits. Worse still it bounces to hit all over again. And again and yet again. It then drags along the ground, encountering the rocks and flints. It goes on encountering them, and dragging – until – until, as with any beast shorn of energy, it finally comes to rest. The people, the inmates of that dragging thing, then realise they are undamaged, but often disarrayed. Or not quite the right way up, whichever way that ought to be. And certainly uncertain of everything just happened. So they start to laugh, and pull at legs, their own or someone else's, before becoming once again the independent human beings that they used to be. Such moments can be delirium, with joy, relief and merriment all equally entwined. The flight itself had been great, and the sights unforgettable, but the landing to conclude the experience does form (in general) the perfect punctuation to the perfect day.

Balloons have now been flying for over two centuries. A strangeness is that they are still a novelty. People, in the main, do stop to watch them. Their clientele, also in the main, still experience the feelings of all their antecedents, the anxiety, the wonder, the pleasure, the delight and fear. It is still a ludicrous and bewitching way to fly. No other kind of aviation comes near its approach to travelling through the air. It was the first method by which humankind could leave the ground without immediately arriving back again. Other forms of flying have been developed since that November day when a manned balloon first ascended in the sky, but many of us will argue that the first way is still the best way. And we expect it to stay that way for years and years to come.

Not quite what the Montgolfier brothers had in mind, but they could have welcomed propane over boots and straw.

CHAPTER 2

The science of ballooning

Joseph and Etienne Montgolfier were quite wrong in their understanding of lift, thinking that some combustible materials were superior in creating buoyancy rather than hot air, and only one of them flew once; but, despite such lack and contradiction, they above all are known as the fathers of aviation.

THE STUDY OF GASES was in its exciting infancy when ballooning began upon its lengthy career. Hydrogen had recently been discovered (by Henry Cavendish) and there was considerable interest in the status of oxygen, particularly since the old phlogiston theory of combustion had been successfully demolished (by the Frenchman, Antoine Lavoisier). However it was an Englishman's book, *Experiments and Observations on Different Kinds of Air* by Joseph Priestley (translated into French in 1776), that allegedly kindled Joseph Montgolfier's enthusiasm for gases. This paper manufacturer (of a 'Royal Manufactory') at Annonay in France tried to repeat some of Priestley's experiments, but failed. Perhaps his scientific comprehension was at fault because his later success, giving him and his brother immortal fame, was founded upon misunderstanding. He believed there was something buoyantly special about combustion products, and certain materials created particularly light gases when consumed by fire. He even decided that damp straw and chopped wool were most suitable, with their generated smoke – rushing upwards – proof of their superiority in creating lightness.

Most strangely it was Britain's determined possession of the Rock of Gibraltar which helped to inspire the birth of flight. In 1782 this strategic outpost had been effectively defended against both France and Spain, much to the irritation of those two countries. Joseph Montgolfier then patriotically proclaimed he had the means for 'introducing soldiers' into the 'impregnable fortress'. His suggestion was a 'large enough bag' to transport 'an entire army above the heads of the English', its lift generated by the combustion of straw and rags. Not only was he therefore proposing the first man-carrying balloon but providing precedent, followed by countless balloonists since his day, for happy exaggeration of potentiality. At all events he and brother Etienne set to work.

These brothers were quite different kinds of individual. Etienne was severely practical, eventually taking over the family's firm. Joseph was the dreamer, the inventor and a perpetual drain on the Montgolfier finances. They made a satisfactory pair, one holding back and the other urging on. As for all the other children – Joseph being the 12th child of Anne

Left: A balloon's envelope must contain its heated air, but there has to be a means for letting that air escape after the landing.

Right: The ripping system must be securely in place at the balloon's apex when inflation is being achieved.

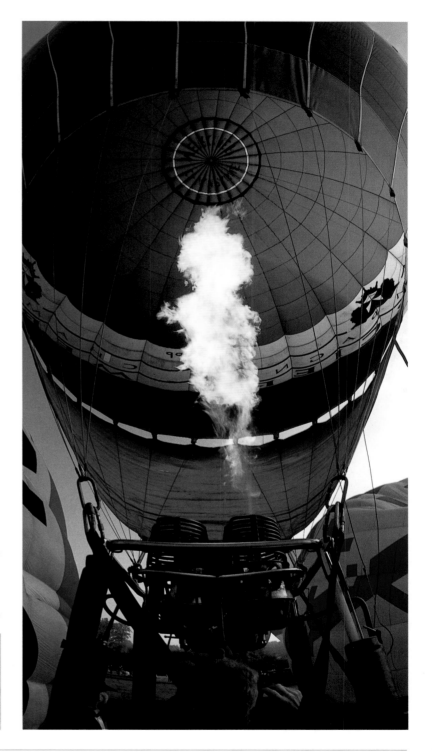

Montgolfier and Etienne the 15th – relatively little is known, but the joint inventors of aviation brought quite sufficient renown on their own towards the family name. One wonders a little about Anne's thoughts concerning this illustrious pair, who were making balloons – of all things, and hurrying to Paris – of all places. She, producing 16 children in 18 years, was surely against such irrelevance with that tremendous family to bring to adulthood. Balloons indeed!

One year after their decision to make a 'large enough bag' the two brothers were at Versailles. Down at Annonay they had constructed bigger and bigger aerostats, all wrong-headedly following the precept that smoke was crucial for creating lift. One Parisian witness later reported that old shoes and decomposed meat were added to the burning straw 'for these are the materials which supply their (lifting) gas'. Reasonably enough, and however intrigued they were by the spectacle, France's King and Queen both withdrew after encountering the noxious smell.

As the world now knows, and was learned by every observer of that first successful flight, the Montgolfier device – however smelly, however wrongly based scientifically – did actually (and most publicly) transport two men for a period of 25 minutes and a distance of 9,000 yards beneath 79,000 cubic feet of heated air. The balloon weighed 1,600 lb, but no one measured its payload – of straw, stoking equipment, damp sponge, and courageous aeronaut. Therefore its internal temperature, either smelling of old boots or with a bonfire's more pleasing fragrance, cannot be assessed.

The effect of the French achievement upon the British scientific community was minimal. Sir Joseph Banks, dictatorial president of the Royal Society, answered a letter of enquiry (and promise of finance) from George III by saying that 'no good' could result from such 'air-globe' experiments as everything was already known which could result from them. The fact that flight had been achieved was therefore of more interest to the (famously mad) king than to the (famously distinguished) scientist. France's Academy (of science) in Paris reacted differently. It was disconcerted that two paper-bag

Left: Propane fuel is still liquid when reaching the burner but, on passing through its coils, is vapourised to be burned with considerable force.

Far right: Propane tanks inside their basket, with a vapour jet indicating that refuelling is near completion. Such containers weigh 70 lb when full.

manufacturers – and from provincial France! – were receiving accolades which should properly be landing in the Academy's lap. After hearing reports from Annonay about the trial inflations it had encouraged a rival enterprise, one to make use of hydrogen rather than hot air. Its unmanned trials were concluded satisfactorily, even if one such aerostat was stabbed with pitchforks after landing near unenthusiastic and belligerent peasantry (who were to become a great deal more belligerent six years later during the revolution).

A mere 11 days after the Montgolfier success from the Bois de Boulogne the Academy team was ready, with Professor Charles at the controls beneath buoyant hydrogen. The two varieties of balloon, hot air and hydrogen, were totally dissimilar in their potentialities. Few aviators subsequently mimicked the Montgolfier approach, with its cloth and paper envelope plus its strange assortment of combustibles. The Charles balloon, by contrast, would not seem greatly out of place if stood beside modern varieties of gas balloon. His 'car' was of wickerwork, his envelope was held captive within a net, his release valve was at the apex, and he even set off trial balloons to check upper winds before his own ascent. The Montgolfier brothers, for all their renown in being first, were quite incorrect in their reasoning. Jacques Charles, *au contraire*, was spot on.

A balloon ascends because its envelope contains something lighter than ordinary air. The substance we breathe weighs slightly over one ounce per cubic foot (or 70 lb per 1,000 cubic feet). The 'something' must therefore weigh less than that amount, and substantially less if lift is still to be available after adding the obligatory weight of envelope for containing that lighter substance. Hydrogen, lightest gas of all, weighs one-fourteenth as much as air, thus creating 65 lb of lift per 1,000 cubic feet. Helium, twice as heavy, provides 60 lb. Coal gas (widely manufactured in the old days) was highly variable but, in general, was less than half air's weight, thus providing some 40 lbs of lift per 1,000 cubic feet. ('Natural' gas, now extensively tapped for domestic use, is unsatisfactory for balloons, being often heavier than air.) The heated air within a modern hot air balloon provides about 17 lb per 1,000 cubic feet, the actual figure depending upon that day's difference between ambient and internal temperature as well as the prevailing atmospheric pressure and the balloon's altitude.

Hot air balloons start their life horizontally, first inflated with cold air (blown from a fan) and then heated until the whole device stands upright, tip-toeing in readiness for the ascent.

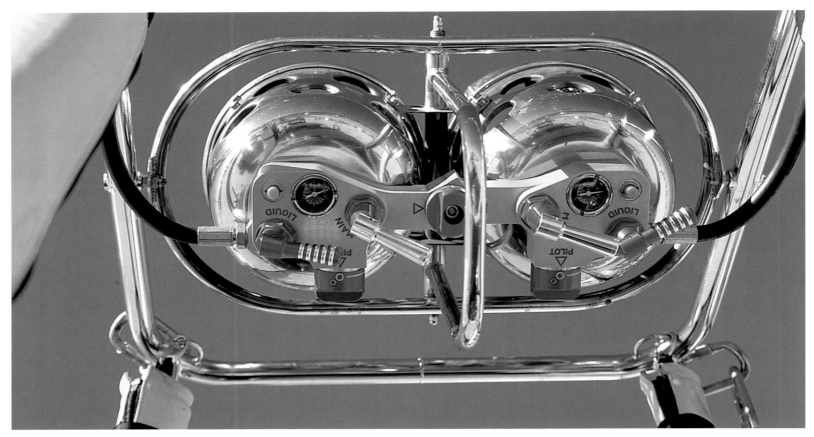

There is a formula governing the lift generated by hot air. If the weight of ordinary air is multiplied by the ambient temperature (in degrees Celsius above absolute zero), and this figure is then divided by the balloon's hot air temperature (also in degrees above zero, this minimum being minus 273 degrees C.), the sum's answer is the weight of the hot air (which must then be subtracted from the weight of normal air). Therefore if the temperature within a hot air balloon is 100 degrees C., if the ambient temperature is 15 degrees C., and if air density is assumed to be 1.2 ounces per cubic foot, the formula reads :

$$\frac{(1.2 \times 288)}{373} = \text{0.28 ounces per cubic foot, or 17.5 lb of available lift per 1,000 cubic feet (7.94 kilos).}$$

In general terms a hot air balloon needs to be about four times larger than a hydrogen balloon to carry the same number of people (with four times 17.5 lb being roughly equal to hydrogen's lift of 65 lb/1,000 cubic feet). Gas balloon fabric, having to contain hydrogen or helium, is several times heavier than hot air fabric (which needs to contain only the large molecules of air). There is much less gas fabric, owing to the gas balloon's smaller volume, but the envelope for, say, a four-man hydrogen balloon is still heavier than for a four-man hot air balloon.

A gas balloonist needs several sacks of sand for each flight, their total weight perhaps 200 lb if those four people wish to fly for three hours or so. A hot air balloonist needs several tanks of propane for a similar flight. The emptied propane tanks are heavier than the emptied sand sacks, and weigh 30 lb each when without propane. In all other respects – basket, instruments and, of course, passengers – the weights involved in the two kinds of balloon are similar. (For individuals who dislike ounces and cubic feet, either for a fondness of the metric system or merely resenting the archaic nature of old style measurements, it is a happy coincidence that the weight of air in ounces per cubic foot – traditionally 1.2 – is virtually the same as the weight of air in kilograms per cubic metre – traditionally assumed as 1.225.)

The two pioneering flights of 1783, so crucial in the history of aviation, are intriguing for yet another reason – the information arising from that famous year does not explain why either aerostat actually left the ground. The Charles balloon was allegedly spherical with a diameter of 27 feet 6 inches. Its volume was therefore 10,500 cubic feet and its gross lift (assuming pure hydrogen) was 682 lb. Its gondola weighed 130 lb, leaving 552 lb for everything else. The weight of Charles and his companion is unknown, but their epic flight took place in December and their combined weight, suitably clothed for the season, was likely to have been in the region of 330 lb, assuming average stature.

Therefore only 222 lb of lift were available for both their envelope (of rubberised silk) and for its embracing net attached to the wooden equator hoop. Such lightness is not impossible, but does stretch the imagination. There was also some ballast on board, stretching it a little further. Consequently it is easy to wonder if the envelope was perhaps larger than reported (with the Paris Academy being a touch perfidious by exaggerating the relative smallness of its favoured aerostat). Modern two-man balloons with much lighter baskets have capacities of about 14,000 cubic feet.

The Montgolfier balloon allegedly weighed 1,600 lb. The two men plus their fuel and stoking equipment must have brought the total assembly to about 2,000 lb. Therefore the heat generated – if those figures are true – would have been higher than the temperatures permitted for modern, propane-fired balloons with heat-resistant nylon fabric. The Montgolfier device is said to have contained 79,000 cubic feet of air. Today's comparable balloon, the popular size of 77,000 cubic feet, produces 1,350 lb (or so) of lift when its contained air is at 100 degrees C. Therefore the 1783 balloon was either subjected to even greater heat (which the cloth/paper envelope managed to survive) or some of the reported measurements are at fault.

Nevertheless the incontestable and all-important fact, witnessed by half (it is said) of the Parisian population at the time, is that both kinds of balloon did fly, did herald the birth of flight, and were astonishing achievements, whether or not the science involved was truly understood and whether or not the actual details were faithfully recorded.

Top left: The pilot's view of a double burner system, with pressure gauges, inlet tubes and throttle handles.

Above right: Instrument panels tend to be modest, being little more – usually – than an altimeter and a rise-and-fall indicator.

Despite this preamble of alleged fact and certain history the science of ballooning can be reduced to a single sentence: Fill a container with something lighter than the air it displaces, and it will become airborne. The science of human ballooning can be similarly reduced: enough air must be displaced by something lighter than that air to offset their weight. As for sport ballooning enough air must be displaced to provide adequate lift not only for maintaining flight but achieving it with extra capacity for safety and control.

Modern development does not alter the fundamental scientific rules, but it can – and has – altered the technology involved. With gas balloons there has been little change, save that fabrics are now lighter and more gas-proof, nets have either been improved or discarded altogether (with fabrics accepting all the load) and valves have been marginally advanced. A crucial fact of gas ballooning, favoured by its loyal enthusiasts, is that change is not entirely welcome. No doubt arquebuses, crossbows, rapiers, coracles and the like could be bettered, but individuals promoting such ancient items are not looking for improvement. They like the old days, the old ways, and in doing so they keep antiquity alive. Gas balloonists (in general) favour tradition, appreciating early methods for their own sake, for their implicit history, for their nostalgia.

Alterations have been attempted but have rarely, if ever, been universally approved. Some new fabrics, undoubtedly efficient as gas retainers, have appeared altogether too shiny, and too modern for general acceptance. Hoops of steel (rather than beautifully laminated wood) have affirmed their better weight/strength ratios, but do look wrong (with their wrongness linked to novelty). The hero of modern hot-air

ballooning, Ed Yost (who so altered thermal flight), has occasionally attempted to transform the ancestral ways of gas.

One day he arrived at a European gas fete with what looked like a can, and lifted this object from his car. Indeed it proved to be a can.

'Does everything from America have to come in cans?' muttered the observing gas traditionalists, all heaving and pulling at considerable weights of bagged envelopes from the backs of several cars.

Left: Approaching touch-down with the hot air correctly enclosed within its envelope.

Above: Touch-down and one form of quick release for all that heated air.

'Wonder what it is,' muttered these gas-men as Ed flipped the lid from his amazing can.

'We know what these are,' they also said, when steadfastly shovelling one ton of sand into 80 little bags for each of their balloons.

'Let's have the gas,' Ed shouted, shortly after he had extracted the contents of his can, thereby providing the sand-bag labourers with happy excuse to halt their heaving, shovelling, and general labouring.

'Where are his bags?,' asked one.

'And his net?' enquired another.

'And his good sense?' demanded a third; 'You need bags and a net if you don't want trouble.'

What Ed did not want was three hours of toil in creating a balloon. Within 20 minutes of his arrival, within 15 of opening that much-derided can, and with its contained polythene inflated fat with the necessary quantity of gas, he was not only ready to depart – but he departed. Shovels, bags, wickerwork, envelopes, sand-heaps, trail ropes, valve nuts, valve lines, ripping-panels and rip lines were all temporarily abandoned as Ed and his shiny-white contrivance ascended peacefully into a halcyon sky. The hope that he might come to grief, and receive appropriate punishment for such insolent effrontery, was almost audible.

As was later heard with disbelief by every gas balloonist, these individuals still at the launching site, his flight had not only been entirely satisfactory but even its aftermath had been unique. Instead of further labour, of the kind the traditionalists knew full well, involving the coercion of heavy fabric back within its bag and much disentangling of net, rope, hook and line, Ed had merely *given* his envelope to the assembled landing crowd. He had torn it into as many pieces as there were pairs of hands, and therefore had no need to fill his empty can. Polythene is cheap, and so are empty cans. He therefore compounded the earlier generosity by giving that away. To the dismay of that day's other gas balloonists, their shirts heavy with sweat and brows much-wiped from half a day's exertion, he was back at the launch-site, virtually empty-handed, before they had taken to the air.

'Just gave it away, did you? And the can? So there was nothing to bring back?'

'Yup,' said Ed, always economical with words.

There have doubtless been other occasions when gas balloonists have taken to the air with mouths agape beneath an assortment of worried frowns. There must have been other times when speechlessness was the order of the day, but I do

not know of these other incidents. I only know, having watched a silent, worried spectacle, that nothing of gas ballooning would, in consequence of Ed's activity, be altered in the years to come. Gas balloonists would continue much as they had always done. Instead of change there would be firm entrenchment, and rather more determination that their ways, the old ways, the only real ways would be maintained as long as possible.

Polythene indeed! Out of a can! And an envelope torn into shreds instead of grunted over, heaved, manhandled and finally embedded within its proper bag. That was how it should be done. And, if the gas balloonists have their say, some of them sufficiently enthusiastic to wear plus-fours, deer-stalkers and other resemblances of earlier days, that is how it will remain.

Gas balloonists can love their far slower but wholly traditional style of preparation, with sand-bags lowered one net-mesh at a time while gas inflates the steadily growing envelope.

CHAPTER 3

The birth of propane man

It is strange that modern hot air ballooning should have been funded initially by the US Office of *Naval* Research, but odder still that this aviation pioneering should have blossomed quite so swiftly and so incredibly abundantly.

FOR MOST OF BALLOONING'S lengthy history a free-flying balloon has been a gas balloon. Admittedly the first ascent used hot air as its lifting medium, and various 19th century endeavours exploited other fuels (wood, oil, petrol) to heat ordinary air, but almost all balloons which flew after the earliest occasion employed a light gas to gain their lift. Hydrogen was the initial choice, although difficult to manufacture, particularly on the spot, but was better by far than actual flame and smoke, particularly if endurance (longer than five minutes) was required.

As the industrial nations developed, and coal gas became most commonplace, there was even less enthusiasm for warming a quantity of air. The light gases then available still caught fire – given half a chance (or less, if they were impure), but they were lighter than any form of heated air and therefore advantageous. By the end of the 19th century, when hydrogen could be encased at pressure within steel cylinders, and every sizeable community had its individual gasworks, there was even less reason for thinking of hot air. Balloons were therefore gas balloons, just as they had (almost) always been.

Think of any famous flight in history (save for that very first) and a gas lighter than air enabled it to happen. The earliest crossing of the English Channel, the first long distance endeavour (London to Germany), the meteorological ascents of the 1860s, the airborne deliverance from besieged Paris, the unfortunate attempt upon the North Pole, and all those jolly Edwardian escapades – they all ascended beneath coal gas or hydrogen. Even in this 20th century, after heavier-than-air flight had taken off (and then took over most of aviation), every balloonist clinging to the ancient sport still clung to gases lighter than air to gain their kind of paradise.

Even when I embraced ballooning (at the start of the 1960s) all my training flights in Holland, the nearest place of instruction then available, were in gas balloons. We inflated with unpleasant-smelling substances brought via our filling tube from pipe-lines running conveniently beneath a patch of tarmac, as in the community of Etten. Its towngas was half the weight of air, and therefore much less light than hydrogen, but it permitted us to become deliriously airborne, time and time again. There was much talk thereafter from other citizens about our acquired and gassy odour, often from be-clogged farmers plainly preferring manure, but never a word or thought that

Balloonists, now familiar with ripping systems, load tapes and the like, should reflect from time to time on the early flying around Sioux Falls which developed their sport so effectively.

heated air might provide an alternative medium permitting buoyant travel over the trim fields, dykes, fences, poplars, barns, bikes, canals and cowpats with which Holland is endowed.

Even in the hostelries afterwards, as we drank deep and neighbours shifted elsewhere, we never imagined that the age-old sport would soon experience revolution. We scraped our shoes and trousers cleaner, laughed, ordered 'noch een' drink, ate 'frites', and wondered where retrieve had gone, but never for a moment imagined propane, nylon, karabiners, and burners belching flame. Quite unknown to us, and over in the United States, the nostalgic pastime which we enjoyed was about to be transformed, to be utterly transformed.

In 1956 General Mills Inc. of Minneapolis received $47,000 to investigate hot air as a lifting medium. Its sponsor was the US Office of Naval Research. It may seem odd – it *is* odd – that the ONR should fund such aerial endeavour, but there was widespread curiosity in the subject and the Navy was first to promote research. A particular interest concerned those pilots forced to descend by parachute over unwelcoming territory or enemy terrain. Instead of using that tested but imperfect method it was thought they might be able to inflate a balloon instead, fill it with hot air, and then hover rather than descend in order – somehow – to be rescued. (Snatching systems were also being devised.) ONR's contract stipulated that its requested hot-air balloon system should be able to carry one man, fly for three hours, reach 10,000 feet and be re-useable. In 1959 several key workers in this enterprise abandoned Minneapolis – and General Mills – to form a separate company (named Raven Industries) in South Dakota, this spot chosen primarily for its lengthy distance to the sea in any direction.

From what material, as prime question, should such a balloon be made? First thoughts were of sheet plastic, but the problem of load stresses quickly ruled out any such product. Second (and better) thoughts were of woven fabric, leading to choice of a nylon known as Flare-cloth. With a tensile strength of 40 lb/inch its weight was a gratifying 0.84 oz a square yard. Unfortunately, being woven, it was porous and needed coating. Therefore a Mylar plastic was laminated to its inner surface, this increasing the fabric's weight to 1.1 oz per sq yd, an acceptable figure.

Into what shape, as further question, should this material be fashioned? To help provide an answer Raven constructed a spherical polyethylene balloon of approximately 27,000 cubic feet. This was inflated with hot air (from an aircraft's heating

unit) and the inverted onion-shape it formed, when lifting 450 lb, was carefully photographed. An envelope of nylon was then fashioned into that – presumably desirable – configuration. To prevent the contained hot air becoming an encumbrance after landing, and to fulfil the role performed by ripping-panels in gas balloons, a 9 ft diameter cylinder of fabric was attached to the open crown. This protrusion would be sealed during flight but promptly opened, via an explosive squib, at touch-down. Then – and only then – all the heated air would be released through a huge and open hole.

Finally, as third major question, what fuel could best supply the necessary warmth? Petrol, paraffin and propane each possess similar quantities of heat potential per pound, but the Raven team quickly disregarded the first two because (as users of Primus and similar camping stoves know full well) such fuels must first be pumped and their burners pre-heated to achieve a decent flame. Propane was therefore selected, its built-in pressure (when kept as a liquid) outweighing its disadvanta-geous need for strong containers.

No thought was wasted on any gondola/nacelle/basket. The propane aeronaut would sit on a single piece of half-inch plywood, this square shape suspended by four steel cables from a load-ring at the balloon's base. As for the actual aeronaut he would be P E Yost (rhyming with toast but Ed for short), chief pilot of more or less everything at Raven Industries, and formerly of General Mills.

In late 1960 an indoor ascent showed that a gross weight of 420 lb (balloon, fuel, rigging, and 190 lb of pilot) could readily be kept airborne, with propane consumption running at 23 lb an hour. Even when an extra 177 lb was added (as potentially disposable ballast) its apex skin temperature never exceeded 220 degrees Fahrenheit, such a heat considered satisfactory for both the nylon and its coating. (The wish for ballast shows that gas balloon procedure was being influential, with sacks of sand a long-standing ingredient for that other form of aviation.)

Sioux Falls, where Raven had its base in South Dakota, is not the most crowded region of the United States; but, for a first trial flight, the Mark I balloon was transported to Bruning, Nebraska, where there lived still fewer people among even less obstruction. Had there been a nearby desert that would probably have been selected, no one knowing at this time how the new hot-air device would actually behave.

The crown line is important for inflation, but can also be used when a balloon is being deflated.

On 21 October 1960, a mere 177 years after the first hot air flight, propane was all ready to take the place of Montgolfier wool and straw. The Bruning inflation was achieved via a Herman Nelson aircraft heater, this process taking 30 minutes. Only when the balloon – ONR X 40 Raven 1 – stood properly upright was the flight burner ignited. Unfortunately, causing instant gloom, the balloon would not then ascend. A modest Nebraskan wind was blowing, presumed (correctly) to be cooling the balloon. Therefore the whole system, envelope + burner + pilot, was walked downwind, this procedure proving successful because the balloon left the ground after little more than 50 feet. Pilot Yost kept the burner working continuously as the balloon ascended to 500 feet. Up there, without any further

action by him, the flight levelled off for 10 minutes. The burner was still operating at maximum power and gradually a descent began. Shortly afterwards, with the flame still burning, a 'landing' was effected. Despite Yost's successful detonation of the explosive squib, he and his plywood seating were dragged 'helplessly across the terrain', according to an official report for the sponsors.

Back therefore to both drawing board and repair shop. The cylindrical 9 ft opening, plainly inadequate, was enlarged to 13 feet in diameter, thus more than doubling its cross-sectional area. The burner, also having proven inadequate, was amended so that propane liquid rather than vapour would be consumed. A metal jacket was fashioned, this containing propane liquid which was then vapourised (by the burner's heat), enabling far more heat to be produced. At Raven they decided, as a basic rule of thumb, that burner capability should be twice that required for level flight. It was plainly unsatisfactory if the burner had to operate continuously. Only if intermittent burning kept the aerostat afloat could ascent or descent be initiated, an impossibility with flight No 1. In short, there had to be a measure of control.

There also had to be as little wind as possible. (Bruning's lightest of breezes had proved this point too clearly.) Therefore, for flight No 2, and only three weeks after that first endeavour, the Raven team and its novel equipment moved to the Stratobowl. This natural volcanic feature in western South Dakota had previously witnessed the launch of many high-altitude balloon flights, its extremely sheltered interior proving ideal. Inflation on this post-Bruning occasion, assisted by a fan, took only six minutes. Take-off was also swifter, and Ed Yost was soon ascending at 400 feet a minute. At 7,000 feet he attempted straight and level flight, a task made harder by the 22 turns necessary to open or close the fuel supply. He then climbed another 2,000 feet but, in attempting further straight and level flying, he encountered violent oscillation, with the balloon ascending and descending uncontrollably.

After 1 hour 50 minutes, and when 39 miles from his starting point, Yost managed a controlled descent. Then, at a comfortable pace of 150 feet per minute downwards, he

The Montgolfier brothers would be totally astonished (and no doubt delighted) by modern burners, with their tremendous ability for generating heat. The venting of propane (left) demonstrates heat loss when it becomes a gas, but coils around the flame ensure a vigorous transformation of liquid into gas, and thus plenty of heat (right) for taking to the sky.

jettisoned 30 lb of ballast, a procedure which would have halted a gas balloon of similar lift from further progress towards the ground, but this act caused 'no appreciable retardation'. A hot air balloon's much greater mass, which includes its contained air, means that various routines satisfactory for gas ballooning could not be universally applied. The transport of ballast by hot air balloon was therefore discarded for good, rather than jettisoned piecemeal when need be as in flying under gas.

Flight No 3, with everyone now bolder, was planned for an airfield near Sioux Falls. Take-off would be achieved, if possible, at a wind strength of 10 miles an hour. When such a day arrived its temperature was a cool 5 degrees F. (minus 15 degrees C.). No ballast was on board, but the pilot had greatly gained in weight from extra clothing. This flight not only started satisfactorily but then proceeded in excellent style. Ed Yost ascended to a planned altitude of 4,000 feet before staying there for one hour. He then descended, calmly and gradually, until reaching 100 feet above the ground. There he remained for another 30 minutes, such evenness of flight being possible now that the 22 turns for adjusting the flame had been replaced by an on/off lever (which had proved its worth at once). As with the flight from the Stratobowl there was again no problem with the landing, the enlarged cylindrical vent having also shown its worth. Flight No 3 had therefore been supreme.

Flight No 4 was to be quite different: no pilot would be on board. Current hot-air balloonists who casually turn off their burners, and who no less casually then descend to some lower altitude, should appreciate that such simplicity was no foregone conclusion. What if the balloon's mouth closed when descending? What if no heat could then be fired (through the fabric) to avert a possibly lethal fall? What if… which was why the fourth flight would be unmanned. A modest 9 lb of fuel were placed on board. Suitable weights replaced the pilot, and telemetry equipment was installed for feeding relevant facts to observers on the ground.

When all was ready, and after a smooth take-off, the balloon ascended to 7,000 feet and there, as planned, the burner failed owing to lack of fuel. Descent then began, but it never became faster than 1,000 feet per minute. No less importantly the mouth stayed open and the balloon's shape remained taut. The

'We're very pleased with the burner', said Ed into the sudden silence, and all subsequent balloonists have reason to be grateful for that propane pioneering.

subsequent landing was abrupt, but not considered lethal had there been a man on board.

ONR X 40 Raven 1 was then officially retired, having suffered in particular from that final touchdown, but also having proved, for the joy of all who fly today, that hot air ballooning was not only feasible but entirely practical. The subsequent Mark II balloon was 38 feet in diameter (as against 40 ft for the earlier version) and therefore contained a volume of 28,500 cubic feet (as against 30,000). Something better than the former seating arrangement was constructed, but only slightly better, the new system being more of a legless camping chair than a rectangle of wood. A drag skirt was added below the balloon's equator, its intended purpose to reduce speed of descent in the event of burner failure. Two propane tanks were then installed by the pilot's shoulders (rather than the former singleton) and the earlier, heavy fibreglass fabric around the mouth (and near the flame) was replaced by more of the nylon of which the balloon was made. The four experimental flights had entirely changed Raven's mood from concerned and wishful thinking to buoyant optimism.

With the arrival of spring in the following year of 1961 all was set to go with Mark II. On 21 March, with Ed Yost again at the controls, this new balloon took off from Sioux Falls and flew most comfortably for 2 hours 20 minutes. As that year progressed a few more modifications were made, with the most important being the introduction of a regulator valve to keep fuel pressure constant. A skirt beneath the mouth was also added to protect the flame from sideways gusts, and the old metal jacket of a vapourisation chamber (for heating the liquid propane) was replaced – because it had split – by a length of stainless steel tubing fashioned into seven coils.

Throughout that year, with flights succeeding modifications and then vice versa, a total of 26 more aerial endeavours were achieved before this phase of operations was concluded on 19 October. Average flight time had been 2 hours 10 minutes. The required altitude had been reached. Mark II was still in good condition, and a message was proudly despatched to the sponsoring Office of Naval Research. 'A low-weight manned flight system capable of safely carrying one man for three hours, at altitudes up to 10,000 feet had been repeatedly flown.'

The propane system had therefore arrived, and propane man had been born. All of us who fly beneath its firm flame today, and beneath the heated air, should give thanks – however strangely this may seem – to the Office of *Naval* Research, and most certainly to Pilot No 1, the man whose name does rhyme with toast and is known to one and all as Ed. He is the hero of all the hours so many of us now spend below a quantity of heated air.

It took time before those events of 1961, so crucial to the modern business of flying beneath hot air, percolated to the world beyond Sioux Falls, and I think I helped them *not* to percolate. During that same year of 1961 a group of us were planning a balloon expedition over Africa. We had always assumed – ever since this errant seed had first begun to sprout – that hydrogen would be our lifting gas. This would be difficult in Africa, with hydrogen supplies sparse (to say the least) and with 10 tons of steel cylinder a transportation problem (again to say the least) for every gas inflation. But what other gas was there? The few European balloonists of that time, the polyglot band of brothers keeping the sport alive, used either coal gas (if near a helpful town) or hydrogen (if near either fat cheque-books or indulgent factories).

Suddenly, having tapped widely for information likely to help our project, we began to hear of South Dakota in general, of Sioux Falls in particular, and of a novel form of aerostat which it was offering. We learned it was a 'thermal device', could be inflated in 10 minutes, had a volume of 60,930 cubic feet, and would take 2-3 men up to an altitude of 10,000 feet for a flight-time of three hours. So was this a good idea for Africa or not? A suitable gas balloon would take three hours to inflate but was one-third of the size. It too could reach 10,000 feet with three people. The purchase price for both systems was about the same – a little over £1,000 – and there were obvious merits in a few tanks of propane rather than a few tons of hydrogen. So what did the European aeronauts think? Did they like the sound of this novel scheme?

In a word their answer was Non, Nein, No. It was new. It had not been tested – much. It was new-fangled, American, metallic, alien to ballooning, and simply incorrect. More to the point, with much of the African landmass over 5,000 feet, with a hotter ambient temperature, and with our need for a minimum crew of three with considerable photographic equipment, we would require a thermal balloon about three times the size they were offering.

'No problem,' wrote back Sioux Falls; 'We will make a balloon three times larger. Just say when.'

In the end it was the lack of a basket which influenced our thinking more than other factor. Every photograph from Raven had shown either Ed sitting on his legless camping stool or a couple of men standing on plywood and holding on to wires. Even in Holland, when brushing through poplars or encountering dykes, I – as proto-pilot – had been grateful for surrounding wickerwork, its creaks and groans all preferable to noises which bodies make on impact. We knew of the 2 inch spines which adorn Africa's yellow-barked acacias, commonest trees in places where we wished to fly. The thought of meeting any tree, let alone the porcupine varieties, when sitting or standing so nakedly filled us with alarm. (And quite rightly, as it happened, for we were later to rasp at 30 miles an hour through some of the nastiest vegetation ever witnessed, the three of us peering at it from deep within our wickerwork protection.)

'Thank you, but no,' was, in brief, the reply sent back to Sioux Falls, South Dakota.

Nevertheless I – as pilot – stayed curious (after Africa) about Raven and their balloons. We did indeed have trouble with our gas balloon and with its cylinders of gas. We had taken 30 tons of them from Britain, and had to shuttle 10-ton quantities back and forth to Nairobi, the only place of hydrogen supply. Each such huge consignment provided the means for one more flight. Perhaps propane would have had merit via its smaller quantities. Perhaps 150,000 cubic feet of hot-air balloon would not have been a greater hindrance than our 27,000 cubic feet of hydrogen. Perhaps I, and the Europeans, had been wrong in our objection to so much novelty. We should, maybe, have been a touch more enterprising.

In 1963, with the African expedition securely in the past, I received word that one of the new-fangled, American, alien and metallic things was coming to England, together with Ed Yost. He – and Raven Industries – had decided that hot-air hops above the American mid-west, however successful, would be more exciting and distinctive over a more impressive hurdle than field after field of corn. From Sioux Falls the next logical step, in Raven's opinion, was the English Channel. This strip of water had achieved ballooning fame 178 years earlier when witnessing the world's first international flight. An American (the financier) and Frenchman (the pilot) had then travelled from England to France to surprise everyone, not least themselves, as no one had flown anywhere in anything less than 59 weeks beforehand.

A single burner is generally sufficient for flight, but the second can be critical when (suddenly) needed, when the ground looms fast, or a tree does, or even another balloon.

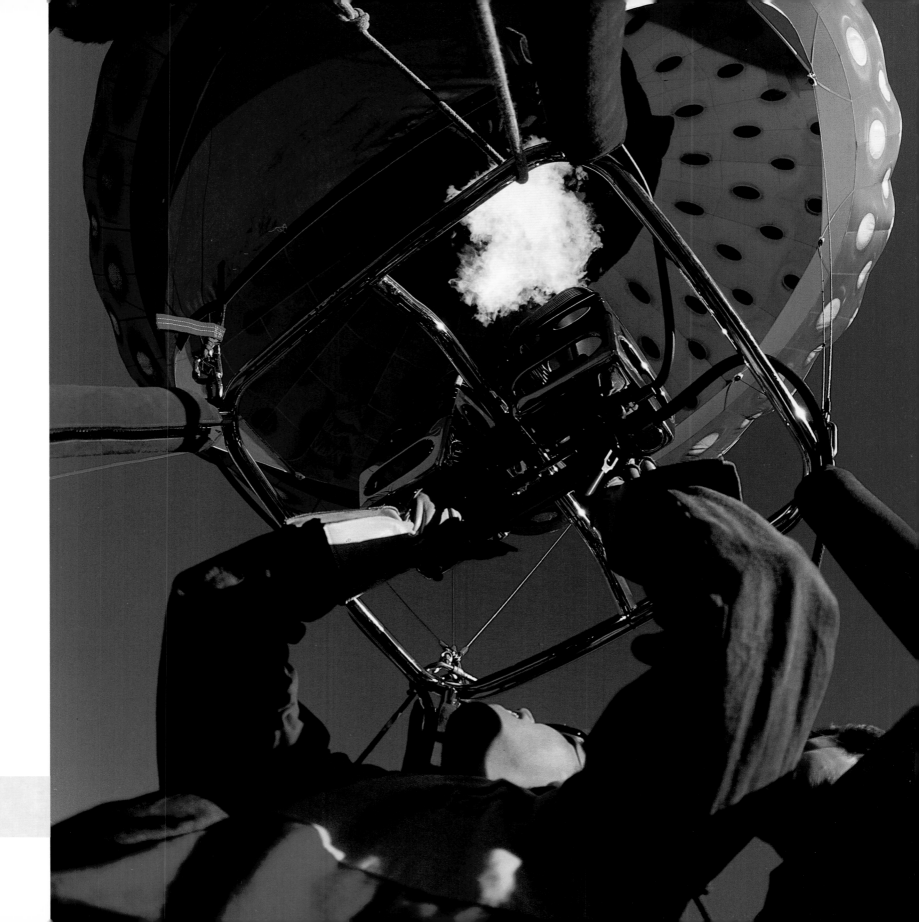

They had provided precedent for subsequent aviators, such as Louis Bleriot who unsettled England's happy insularity by flying a monoplane from France in 1909, and then – 54 years after his achievement – by such as Ed Yost who intended to demonstrate that quite another form of flying had arrived. He and his contrivance would show to a wider audience what had been achieved back in South Dakota.

A team of five eventually arrived with the novelty. Don Piccard, whose father, mother and uncle had done extraordinary things by way of ascent and descent, was to be co-pilot with Ed. Their meteorologist would be Emily Frisby. She too worked at Raven but had an Englishness (apart from her birth and upbringing) which no American could ever hope to emulate (or, indeed, could many of her fellow UK citizens). J R Smith was in charge, and R A Pohl had also arrived to lend a further pair of hands. Initially, as prior test, they inflated their pure white balloon within No 2 hangar at Cardington, before departing to check the Kent and Sussex coast for a suitable launch pad.

Once they had seen the old cinque port of Rye they looked no further, this town lying directly (and protectively) above some flat land (which had been English Channel not so long ago). The area looked ideal, and so did the George Hotel, a place of beams, brasses and general antiquity with no equal among the taverns of Sioux Falls. Having ensconced themselves, and having made customary comment about perfidious plumbing, low ceilings and odd speech, they settled to enjoy warm beer and alien food while waiting for suitable wind. Emily would tell them when it might arrive.

They also learned I was on their trail. As Britain's solitary private balloonist at that time I felt, in part, I should be host to their endeavour, or at least say 'Hello'. In greater part I longed to become better acquainted with the flying machine I had rejected and also, no less importantly, to learn how it created the quantities of heat to keep aeronauts aloft.

'Oh, you'd like to see the burner, would you?' answered Ed after I had located Rye, the George, and the group from South Dakota.

We moved to the hotel's garage and found what resembled a trio of large springs. There were also rubber tubes, thin fabric in a bag, a length of tape, and a wooden platform with two shiny tanks. Could this assemblage be a balloon, and was that all? Following a short hiss, and Ed's suggestion that I should stand

It may have handling ropes, foot-steps, a padded rim and straps for fixing propane tanks, but a wicker basket is still crucial for ballooning's form of flight.

more distantly, there was sudden and tremendous noise – plus immediate pain at the back of my head. Reflex actions have a place in human survival but can be damaging if cross-beams are solidly nearby. As for the flame I had never seen such external combustion. The thing was six feet long, one foot wide and of every colour, but on that evening and within that modest garage it was noise that most bewildered. Even open exhausts of aeroplanes had never seemed so loud.

'We're very pleased with the burner,' said Ed into the subsequent silence; 'We think it'll get us across.'

Came the day, or rather came the darkness long before dawn following a warning call from Emily. The date was 13 April 1963. I reached Rye from London together with the daylight. All five of them were busy, and I took opportunity to look at what they called their gondola. I would have called it a plank, a curved plank seven feet long and four feet wide. It had no sides, save for a modest circumferential tape about a foot above the woodwork. This could only serve to mark the edge rather than restrain an aeronaut from tumbling overboard.

'We can hang on to the tape if things get real bad,' said Ed who saw me looking.

'Yup, good to have a bit of tape,' said I, wondering what things he had in mind.

The team then initiated the procedure, witnessed by me for the very first time, which every modern hot-air balloonist now knows so well. They lit their monstrous flame. They encouraged its heat within the envelope and very soon (ludicrously soon, from a gas balloonist's viewpoint) they were ready to depart. Ed and Don sat on the two shiny propane tanks, these lying sideways on the wooden platform, and Don explained how the floor's curved shape would help them toboggan on the ground at landing time. Two of the four supporting wires would be disconnected, enabling the expiring envelope to drag the platform horizontally until friction called a halt. An exploding squib would simultaneously open up the crown, thus releasing air and helping to end the flight.

I have no photo of me that day, but any such memento would have shown a face wrinkled both with disbelief and anxiety. I felt a deep nostalgia for the proven virtues of sand-bags, trail-ropes, wicker and rope. The converse picture of tanks, plank, stainless steel and a 6-ft flame seemed awesome substitute. I also felt no longing to be on board.

'Anyone got a match?' asked Don merrily after Ed had turned a tap from full to trickle, causing a sudden vanishing of flame.

Various individuals took him at his word, offering boxes and lighters. Their faces were, like mine, puckered with concern. Should they, by offering matches, be condoning the adventure and providing encouragement for such a lethal scheme? Or should they attempt restraint, not wishing to be witness to an enterprise the like of which they had never seen before?

Then, quite suddenly, the two aeronauts were off. Ed had turned the tap to full again, Don's chat had been drowned in

the burner's roar, and we on the ground were gazing at the plank from underneath. Our early morning crowd of 30 assorted insomniacs from Rye were the sole witnesses to a historic departure. The time was 7.45 am. The wind blew from the west and was therefore, although more northing would have helped, set sufficiently fair for France. We watchers waved and waved, as is the compulsion, and the two of them occasionally waved back. We certainly wished them well in their endeavour, whatever things might come to pass and what fate possessed in store.

Later we learned, not without relief and even astonishment, that they had landed near Gravelines, half way between Calais and Dunkirk. In flight they had ascended to 12,000 feet and had travelled 65 miles in 3 hours 17 minutes before their safe touchdown slightly to the north of due east of Rye. I had written of the impending flight for the *Daily Telegraph*, but this paper proved uninterested in its accomplishment.

'Not if they didn't die, or at least get hurt,' said the news editor, type-cast of his breed; 'Didn't they even get a little wet? What kind of a flight is that!'

The event also failed to shake the aviation world, but the fact did slowly penetrate that American thermal balloons were viable propositions. Hot air ballooning *was* feasible. There *was* an alternative to the expense of gas ballooning. Aerostation *could* be achieved without a regiment of sand-bags and half a day of preparation. The world did not immediately beat a path to Raven's door, any more than it had hurtled to Kitty Hawk after the Wrights had shown what could be done with sound theory, one engine and four good wings. These things take time, or so it seems. Pioneers are ahead of the game. They have to wait awhile for others to catch up, and only then – perhaps – can those others overtake.

Hot air balloons, and their balloonists, have witnessed much innovation since the modern resurgence begun by Raven in those early 1960s. There is no particular nostalgia, either for Montgolfier's wool and straw or for Ed Yost's earliest device, however crucial these differing advances in the promotion of balloons. Similarly no one much liked his toboggan style of landing, with two wires detached and two remaining wires taking all the strain. Keeping all four wires attached remained preferable, however attractive the notion of skidding along the ground. Neither was the apical opening much approved,

A Raven pilot (right), with two propane containers keeping him company, testing the fuel which has powered (left) the resurgence of ballooning.

however wide its diameter and reliable its explosive bolts. It may have been effective, preventing Ed from further drags 'helplessly across the terrain', but once it had been opened and exploded there was no redress. It could not be re-sealed. Therefore the flight would, upon that instant, come to an end, most assuredly, even if the pilot then had a change of mind. The point of no return (to happy altitude) would have been encountered at that very moment the opening had been made.

(Or perhaps there was different reason for that opening's abandonment. The thought of any system, however secure, being such an immediate arrangement for losing every particle of lift, could have had many a pilot incapable of relaxation. What if, say at 10,000 feet…? What if, say at 20 feet…? Losing two supporting wires, however inadvertently against an allegedly fail-safe system, would be bad enough at height, precipitating occupants without delay. Losing all the lifting

medium, with equal unintention, would be no more satisfactory – and possibly rather less. Perhaps Ed could sleep at night with such arrangements, but others might find that wakefulness becomes more dominant.)

Nevertheless there had to be some procedure for releasing air, its vital support becoming encumbrance when the landing had been achieved. At first Velcro solved the problem. Two attached surfaces could be torn apart and then, when the pulling ceased, they could become – to some degree – re-attached. Mud – the inevitable mud of landings – increases its inefficiency, and one horrific accident (killing two) when some wet and old Velcro yielded under strain prompted further thinking. There had to be a better way.

Since those days all sorts of better ways have been devised, all uniform in permitting the pilot to re-seal the opening. In general the hot air itself helps with the closure, its upward thrust providing the necessary force. These deflation systems have been circular or triangular, their sealing has been 100 per cent or rather less, and they have involved many rigging lines or very few. Despite (or because of) the steadfast addition of so much novelty they have done well.

As for burners and their fuel supplies the single uniformity is that they still – like Raven in 1960 – have propane as the source of energy. As for their outputs these have changed dramatically. When Malcolm Brighton and I were devising the first home-grown burner, learning about flame speed (and once filling his entire driveway with a cloud of propane vapour) the experts were informing us that 2 million BTUs – our desired quantity – could not be created by our solitary burner (one BTU being the heat required to heat 1 lb of water through 1 degree F.). We did create such heat – just, flew over power lines – just, and could even turn off the burner during flight – momentarily, but we knew improvement in output would be helpful. However we never knew, or even imagined, that modern double burners would be rated at 24 million BTUs, a 12-fold leap enabling balloonists to escape no end of trouble.

Burner noise is still a problem. Many a balloon passenger refers to the silence of aerostation, and perhaps intermittent silences do become more memorable after deafening squirts of noise. The manufacturers, aware of this drawback, use words like stealth and whisper for their propane torches. Other words like mute, hush, pin-drop and mime are – perhaps – just around the corner. Gas balloonists, forever aware of basket creaks, of rope-eyes tightening, and of bird-song down below, tend to call the other balloons noisy, loud, stentorian, thunderous by comparison with their aphonic form of flight. Save that gas balloonists, aware of gentle decibels, so often add to them with cat-calls and jovial bombast as they too travel through the air, affirming all the while their quiet superiority. On reflection honours are about even between the Charlies (as they are sometimes called) and the Montgolfiers.

One noise mercifully absent these days is an exclamation, generally from the tallest basket-member, of dismay that the burner assembly has hit him on the head. When ropes or wires formed the sole connection between basket and burner frame there was a tendency, indeed a momentum obligation, that basket contact with the ground should immediately be followed by burner contact with someone's cranium. Fortunately there are now flexible poles of nylon as well as wiring between basket and burner. The tallest can now stand tall, rather than shrink in anticipation when landing time arrives. The shortest can also be relieved that a fearful, deafening oath will not shatter their ears following a basket's reunion with Mother Earth (or mother rock, or mother dry-stone wall).

It is still a basket in which aeronauts ascend. In former times wicker-weave was considered ideal, being the best material available for strength, lightness, and general resilience. It would bend, if need be, and could yield sympathetically. Each basket's rectangle would become diamond-shaped on impact rather than inflict damage upon its clientele. The chosen osiers seemed physically in keeping with the human frame, and many a savage contact with ground (or rock or wall) would have passengers astonished that they could stand on two good legs, let alone walk away (while laughing) from the landing site. Modern baskets still look like baskets (and *are* baskets) but are made of sterner stuff. The floors are of multi-ply-wood, and the sides have a log-cabin approach to all the wicker-work. All items are strong, purposeful and capable of bearing friends, punters and propane in considerable quantity, but the wish for rectangles ever to become diamonds has plainly receded in the face of modern needs.

But – and this must be the major point – people expect conventional balloons to have wicker baskets (however solidly), just as they expect champagne (however sparkling). They also anticipate silence, so much so that they will merrily speak of it with voices hoarse from happy chat during the burning time. Finally they know, this knowledge embedded for all time, that a balloon's ascent may be exciting, stimulating and even rewarding, but its ultimate descent will be doubly, trebly so because it forms certain prelude to the landing.

Balloon flights are all very well, but their eventual touch-downs (or thump-downs) are icing on the cake, even if – or notably if – the cake is delivered either sideways on or upside down. In this particular perspective they are absolutely right. Basket-weave may not be as it used to be, or the silence, or the bottles (or cans!) of bubbly, and modifications will endlessly be applied to balloons, but their landings will continue to be as they have always been: erratic, distinctive, horrific, amusing, astonishing and entirely memorable, being wholly apt conclusions to quite delicious days.

CHAPTER 4

The joy

Aircraft steadily took over the skies since first becoming airborne 120 years after ballooning's prime ascent, but balloons are now staging a major comeback, with more of them flying today than ever before in their lengthy history.

BALLOONS ARE UNDOUBTEDLY ARCHAIC – nothing else has a longer history concerning human flight. They are a touch pointless – no other conveyance, save for a raft, offers its occupants less authority over their destination. They are huge, being at least one cubic foot in size for every ounce they carry. They do not come cheap, and never did. They can also kill, with the first aviation casualties occurring less than 19 months after the prior aviation. And yet, most astonishingly, the pastime of ballooning is currently the fastest growing form of flight. There are more balloons and balloonists today than in all their lengthy history. Of the registrations of new aircraft added to the civil list each year a huge proportion is of balloons.

Archaic, rudderless, large, costly, sometimes lethal, and increasingly popular! They were thought amazing when they first ascended in the air. They are still thought astounding, a fact to be coupled with the greater surprise that their popularity is gaining more speedily than ever. The early bewilderment is understandable, in that no one had ever become airborne previously – save for a few flapping individuals, leaping from towers or bridges, who either did or did not survive their return to earth. The current and expanding affection for ballooning is occurring in a world where aviation is commonplace. We now, as like as not, go on holiday by air. We visit cousins in Australia, business partners in New York, and our offspring wherever they have settled down. The superior speed of aircraft has enabled them to kill off liners and, no less competitively, they have also injured trains. They are paramount in war, and therefore loom large in every budget. Even our sunny skies are often interlaced with the trails of aeroplanes, and the entire 20th century has been revolutionised, largely from the air.

In the midst of all this aerial activity there are balloons. For their first 120 years the aerostats had the heavens entirely to themselves. No one else was up there to harm them (or for them to harm). There were no control zones, telling them where flying was permitted (and where forbidden). Similarly the ground was formerly free of electricity, and not supporting a wirescape of 220 volts – or even, where they march across the land, pylons carrying voltages a thousand times as strong. Such deterrence seems to have made balloonists yet more determined – to find free airspace, to avoid rivals, to discover landing space between all the obstacles.

Finally, as most potent fact of all, Britain has the greatest

Whether within the Avon Gorge near Bristol, or over factories, swamps, towns, forests, hills, dales or whatever, a flight by balloon is like none other.

agglomeration of balloon enthusiasts, per square mile of countryside, (same for miniature Luxembourg), than any other nation. This might be comprensible if Britons were less exposed to unkind weather than other nationalities, if anti-cyclonic calm was standard for most days, and if gales, fog, rain or miserable visibility were extreme rarities. Instead, with the British Isles anchored, as it were, within the Atlantic Ocean, and with that ocean home to some of the planet's foullest weather forms, its cyclonic systems invade the first land they encounter with gay impunity. By no meteorological yardstick is Britain highly suitable for ballooning, but by no reasonable form of judgement are Britons lavishly endowed with common sense. Their country is a very windy, rainy place. Wind and rain are each unsatisfactory for ballooning. Therefore – with the kind of rationale only sensible within the United Kingdom – Great Britain has become Number One ballooning country, per head of population and per possible landing place, of all the countries in the world.

A greater question concerns the ballooning resurgence as a whole. There are answers of a sort – commercial flying has reduced aviation to zero pleasure – advertising can help to pay for balloons – light aircraft had their heyday in the '20s and '30s – but there is one other which deserves particular mention. Balloons are forgiving. They tolerate error. They do not obey the ordinary, harsh, and demanding ways of flight. Their category is their very own. They look odd, and are odd. Even their problems cannot be judged correctly.

No one laughs when some heavier-than-air machine is blatantly in trouble, but if a balloon has a problem, and is either heading for a tree or is already badly flawed, the event is often seen as some kind of comedy turn, a clown on a banana skin, an antic good for ribaldry. Perhaps the observers, clutching their sides with happy pain, are quite correct in their assessment. A balloon can be in trouble, in terrible trouble, and then get away with it. It can land on a roof, in a truck, on rock, in swamp, or on telephone wires and become enmeshed. 'Please tell the president,' shouted a ballooning friend (who knew, as did the crowd below, whose wires they were), 'that Alan Root is on the line'.

Even when some mishap is proceeding its impending accident can induce less fear within the basket than should arise. No one jests when an aircraft's engine goes quietly dead, or smiles when some wrongful noise interrupts that awesome quiet, but

equivalent happenings with a balloon can, and probably will, lead to a quip or two. Balloonists are no more courageous than other kinds of aviator but know, from personal experience and all the history, that a balloon is not a vengeful thing, rich with metal and cutting edge. It permits its occupants to survive – if possible, and probably without a single scratch to mark the incident.

Take the day in Belgium, for example, when failing ropes ought to have caused death (at the very least). And would certainly have done so had the aircraft in question been of a heavy kind when equally short of its control. Our departure from the city square of St Niklaas had been delayed. (There were reasons, such as hurrying to Holland to collect a forgotten net, but they were not relevant, save in consuming time.) A dozen other gas balloons were ascending as we returned and, following each of their departures, we worked more frantically with ours, cutting corners, knowing time was short, and longing to be airborne. Suddenly, as is the nature of speedy take-offs, I and one bean-pole of a Belgian named Didier were hurtling upwards, having happily left all confusion down below.

It was then a perfect evening. Our sweat evaporated and our thirsts also disappeared as we drank deep from various bottles on board. Everything was as it should be, with the flatness of Flanders looking both flatter and better still from our 2,000 feet. There was no need to read a map, my passenger knowing the land beneath, and it was all tranquillity. Didier and I relished the experience of watching the passing scene, he for the first time and I as content as ever with this form of travel through the air.

Of course perfection never lasts and, after a couple of hours, we accepted that our flight would have to be curtailed, the late start having shortened possibilities. Therefore I pulled on the valve line to release a portion of our buoyant gas, and received some 50 feet of rope upon my head.

'Is that a problem?' queried Didier, uncertain about ballooning but suspecting that pilots should not become embroiled, Laocoon-like, in 50 feet of rope.

I admitted we had encountered a set-back, there now being no means of arranging our descent.

'Then the flight will become even more interesting?' suggested my companion with 20/20 vision. I agreed out loud, but not within. Although unnerved by a situation never before experienced I was comforted (slightly) by Didier's calm (as he

The antics of ballooning are often misunderstood by observers, but who can blame them if they have just seen a strawberry bigger than the trees.

steadily pointed out some area he knew). It is also difficult to panic (at least out loud) when standing in a wicker basket, bathed in sunshine, and replete with drink and chocolate bar. Even so I did wonder which portion of ground the fates had in store as a final landing place – that smoking factory, those power lines, or that clover-leaf of cars. Normally, when a good field is in view and straight ahead, a pull on the valve line will lower the balloon into that field, but normally a balloon's pilot is not enmeshed in coils and twists of rope as he focusses on a roadway's convolutions. Or on lengthy, hanging, humming, and lethal strands of wire. Or merely on a busy place of manufacture, set about with glass and iron and oily drums.

In the end the landing was exquisite. Our contained gas had gradually cooled as the day had cooled, and equally gradually we had neared the ground. To my amazement a perfect grassy field then loomed as our resting place, and into it we dropped, gently, calmly, and entirely perfectly.

'There was no problem,' said bean-pole Didier, unravelling the rest of me; 'What more must we now do?'

Having done absolutely nothing (save worry) since pulling down that faulty rope I was eager for activity. Therefore I pulled sharply on the only other rope, the control line for releasing all the gas; but then once more I was embroiled. The 50 feet of rip-line fell about me as the 50 feet of valve line had done in the earlier episode.

'Another problem?' queried Didier, learning fast about ballooning but still uncertain if ropes tended to act this way.

I explained, as some 20,000 cubic feet of gas stayed buoyantly above us, that there was now no way for releasing any of it. Plainly the ropes had suffered from damp, or general rot, to part so easily. Equally plainly I had no idea what next to do, the valve being some 60 feet above our heads at the highest point of our balloon.

'Difficult to reach,' I informed my companion who, very tall and thin, was still a long way short of the necessary goal.

'We need a ladder,' said Didier, his mind racing.

'Archaic, rudderless, large, costly, sometimes lethal, and increasingly popular. They were thought amazing when they first ascended… They are still thought astounding…'

'A long ladder,' he added, getting to grips with the task.

'Now who has very long ladders?' he wondered, his eyes shining brightly.

'I know, I know,' he exulted, 'we'll call the fire brigade.'

'You can't do that,' I responded tediously. 'They're only interested in – well – fires.'

There was a small garden shed in view, a collapsed thing not worth much more than the several nails still holding it together. I suggested putting a match to it before we summoned aid.

Then, that conflagration extinguished, we could suggest a ladder's loan as the firemen prepared to leave. Didier dismissed my concern at once, asked someone to call the emergency service, and very soon we heard a siren hurtling down the nearby road. One enormous vehicle then halted and firemen sprang from every pore. A few approached us, asked for guidance and I, softened by their zeal, muttered about a ladder being of considerable benefit.

They were delighted, they said, to be of assistance. Their vehicle immediately extruded pods from all four corners, blocked the traffic in both directions and began to raise its lengthy ladder. Embarrassment can, on occasion, become so overwhelming it is no longer embarrassing. The developing situation could only be savoured, particularly as I (knowing how to dismember valves) would have to be installed in a small cage at one end of the ladder now being swung into position. After bringing the balloon near the huge, road-blocking appliance I climbed into its metal container, together with one colossal firemen who only spoke in grunts. The two of us soon soared aloft, with someone far below controlling our ascent. This occurrence was hardly ballooning, but the view quickly became the one I had remembered from our earlier descent.

While I and grunt-man stood and watched, those on the ground manoeuvred the ladder so

that the balloon's valve lay directly beneath us, with our straight and extended ladder unable to reach the apex of a sphere. No sooner had I seen this difficulty than, with yet another gentle growl, my companion protruded a smaller ladder from beneath our cage. Down this I climbed before swiftly unclipping the valve's connections which kept it sealed. That done I was immediately bathed in a torrent of hydrogen, a draught which took my breath away.

Indeed it did. I turned to shout to my accomplice, knowing the balloon would increase in height (and damage itself on all that iron) when its sphere became more vertical.

'Up a bit,' I yelled.

At least it was meant to be a yell. One trouble with hydrogen, the least dense gas of all, and one trouble with lungfuls of the stuff, is that yells thenceforth are quite impossible. Instead every intended shout is nearer to a squeak than proper vocal sound. My fireman friend, so guttural in his own deliberations, could not believe his ears. He stared and stared while I just squeaked and squeaked.

He could no more take his eyes off me than I could make a decent noise, and there we were transfixed, Flemish grunter, English cheeper, not knowing where to turn. While I was awash with hydrogen he was greatly stunned with curiosity.

Then, after seeing the balloon's problem for himself, he fog-horned to down below, and soon the two of us (with all our iron) were swung aside to safety. In that clear air I inhaled gulp after gulp. Eventually, having checked my system with a little cough, I was ready to readdress that large companion. Lowering my chin, and deepening my voice an octave or two (a trick learned at puberty), I rumbled out some words.

'Dank u zeer. Merci monsieur. Merci. Dank.'

This further transformation astonished him all over again. I swear I could hear his brain working as the two of us were lowered to the ground. He walked to his colleagues as if dazed, while even his grunts had gone. As for Didier he was overjoyed and full of praise.

'Ballooning is great. Please another such aerial voyage. Soon. Perhaps tomorrow?'

Yes, ballooning *is* great. It lets you get away with it, time and time again. Didier looked taller still as he laughed with friends about the flight. He was not dead. Nor did he have a single scratch as memento of the day. He had flown in a balloon, and

Albuquerque in New Mexico is the acknowledged balloon capital of the world, notably during October at its annual jamboree.

the balloon itself was equally unscathed. Best of all, as I had feared quite differently, the firemen never even sent a bill.

My personal ballooning experiences had begun over Holland, where I had learned the trade, but it was in Africa that I had learned how little I knew. It was there that I had flown in charge for the very first time, and there is nothing like being in charge for learning at quite a different level. No one else makes the mistakes. No one else can be blamed. And there is no one else who learns so rapidly, the faults hammering home their messages more loudly than to anyone else on board. I once took off at midday – which was fatuous, with Africa then at its hottest, with thermals building up their energies most terrifyingly. I also took off in places where the scenery was good, which meant cliffs, hills, and escarpments all designed to tie air-flows into knots.

These balloon flights had left me personally amazed that I had physically survived, still sound of wind and limb, but my mind had not been so unscathed. Being, as on one occasion at 9,500 feet, without a morsel of sand remaining (to serve as brake) for the inevitable plummet downwards, lingered in my memory. It is true we had drink and food on board, and our shoes, and camera equipment, each to be jettisoned when that time came, and they did much to diminish our descent – notably the heavy 500 mm lens which was dropped most merrily, and it is also true we did survive, but it was a tree that had saved us most of all.

A tree is wonderfully made for balloonists. First contact on descent is with twigs which yield to sprigs, limbs, branches, and boughs, each of greater firmness than their predecessors. To hit the boughs first would be most damaging. To hit them when decelerated by the earlier elements is infinitely better. The black and ancient tree on which we dropped did serve us perfectly. It not only stopped our fall but then rejected us, its bent limbs plainly wishing to regain their normal stance. That bounce threw us to another tree, and from it we cascaded – almost gently – to the ground. I do not know what the others did, but I know I lay there, face upwards, eyes shut, bewildered how we had survived.

Back in England I rolled the bagged balloon into my home, rolled it within a cupboard rarely used, and shut the door most purposefully, as if some wild thing was inside. As for the basket, too big for entrance, I put it in the garden, encasing it with the rubber sheathing we had placed beneath it before floating above the straits of Zanzibar. I had doubted that sheath's benefit, had we touched down in the sea, but it was perfect for diverting British rain – and enabling me to forget, as far as possible, the terrifying times which it and I had shared.

Over in Holland and Belgium, where I had acquired not only my balloon but the *Bewijs van Bevoegdheid als Ballonvoerder* which had permitted me to fly it, they expressed curiosity about the African venture. Had the balloon truly escaped undamaged? Had I? 'Why not come over to Dongen for the next *ballonfeest* and let us have a look at both of you?' The idea struck me as ridiculous. Even the name of Dongen had a bell-like noise, the tolling of a knell which had already sounded, much too frequently, in my ears. Of course I could not go.

'We have reserved you a fine hotel,' they informed me two weeks later.

'By which transport are you coming,' they requested later, 'so we can give you our assistances?'

'Everything is arranged,' they added later still; 'It only needs, how you say, your say so.'

So I said so, and then wondered why. As it happened the occasion was to restore my faith in ballooning absolutely. There were Albert, and Jo, and Alfred, and Nini, and Pamela, and Hans, and Jacques, and Ben, and Jean, and François, and Charles – all laying out balloons, all chatting merrily, all lending each other a hand, and then eventually ascending in basket-loads without a care in the world. I too took off and watched my aerial colleagues flying low to chat with farmers, trumpeting at each other, laughing audibly, jettisoning sand from time to time, and never hurtling up to 9,000 feet before, when hurtling downwards, discarding bottles of drink, sandwiches, camera film, or a lens of any weight. From Dongen, now with a happier ring, we eventually each landed, haphazardly of course, but all most joyfully.

As a consequence, with my confidence merrily restored, I accepted invitations to fly in England, to 'be the high spot of our summer fete, itself the high spot of each year', to 'commemorate the new church roof', to 'send our Lady Mayoress into the heavens but not, we hope, permanently'. The flights were fun, and England always looked terrific. Its air currents were gentle, never mimicking the vicious thermals of midday Africa. The clientele on board were enthusiastic, whatever their earlier experiences of airborne travel.

'Done much flying?' I would enquire.

'Never been higher than a brick wall,' was one reply.

Modern fabrics accept modern colouring, and balloons these days are nothing if not exuberantly exhibitionist.

Sadnesses were few, such as the time when one enormous councillor, longing to fly, had to be replaced by his trim, charming and younger secretary, one third his weight.

The balloon *Jambo*, christened with this word for 'Hello' on the maiden voyage, brought to light many ancient memories. 'There was a balloon here in 1926, you know. Fellow named Willows flew it. He died, you see, when he hit a tree.' At Malmesbury I learned not only of a monk who had, allegedly, attempted to fly in mediaeval times from the Abbey's tower, but of its balloonist MP who had ascended from his constituency on a blustery 10 December 1881, had not fallen out as the two others did when they hit a field near Bridport on the Dorset coast, and was last observed heading south over a stormy sea. *Jambo* was the first privately-owned, man-carrying balloon to be seen over Britain for more than three decades. It therefore helped (as happy evocation of earlier times) to extinguish memories of World War Two when British skies were only filled with belligerent forms of aviation, either theirs or ours.

It was easiest to enjoy most of all the flights with other forms of aviator on board. 'But why isn't the thing stalling?' demanded an ancient fixed-wing pilot, most unhappily, having flown in almost everything else (and no doubt having stalled in quite a few of them). Two V-bomber men, accustomed to leaving East Anglia almost the moment they took off, were astonished that flight could be so different and – let it be said (as they did) – rather more enjoyable. From Dunstable I once ascended with five glider pilots on board. Their cries were pitiable to hear when *Jambo*, had it been a glider, would have been in terrible trouble, so low to the ground, so much in need of thermic lift, so certain to hit those trees. As it was I jettisoned a handful of sand, waited while anguish turned to mute astonishment, and then overcame those trees, perhaps by a couple of feet, perhaps by not so much.

One way and another, either for being flown or because they had witnessed an ascent, or descent, or subsequent pub assembly, various individuals let it be known that they too would like to be a pilot, or at least involved with free-flying balloons. I would write down their names and then, as like as not, do nothing more to aid their aspiration, save wonder what I should be doing on their behalves and why only those particular individuals had expressed an interest. Perhaps fishermen or golfers, stamp collectors or vintage car devotees, are equally disparate, but I could see no unifying factor among those whose names I added to the list. Old, young, large, small, wealthy, blatantly impoverished, aviation-minded or at first base in this regard, there seemed no rhyme or reason why they, and

not others, had expressed such enthusiasm for the sport of lighter-than-air.

When one group of individuals decided (during those 1960s) to build a hot-air balloon, the first propane device to be manufactured in Britain, I could still see no concordant pattern in their lives thus far. They called themselves the Seven-Up, and were – a cider manufacturer, a press photographer (interested in canal boats), an ex-needle-bearing salesman (delighted to be ex), an oil company executive, an agent for French car-lights (who spoke all sorts of languages, and had been in Wellingtons during the war), an aeronautical engineer (which did make sense), and a man addicted to gliding. Very quickly their varied provenance mattered not a scrap, with the rest of us speedily knowing them as Giles, Tom, Malcolm, Bill, Charles, Don, and Mark.

As for the growing list of other hopefuls, often scribbled absent-mindedly, this not only lengthened but soon became a pile of letters. 'You will remember that we met/I helped you with your sand-bags/We pulled you from the swamp/You promised to get me airborne.' These letters then gave way, as unanswered correspondence often does, to further letters, up an octave or two in tone. 'I cannot understand why... Please be so good as to... Surely you can find a stamp... We await impatiently.'

Plainly, if there was not to be a further shift in emphasis, another hike in style, the time had come for something akin to action on my part. Three years and six months after the return from Africa, having stimulated but not satisfied, and having watched the 'Balloonists' file swell from thin to embarrassingly unwieldy, I drafted a brief and single letter for duplication to all concerned:

You have expressed an interest in lighter-than-air, and are therefore invited to a meeting on November 30th, 1965, which will he held within the Royal Aero Club. The purpose is to discuss the possible formation of a club dedicated to l-t-a in general and ballooning in particular.

If people wanted to go ballooning it was up to them to do something. The buck, as I saw it, was about to leave my hands. Came the day and 90 individuals turned up at the Royal Aero

Deflation after touch-down. One person, and then another (left), pull on the crown line. Hot air escapes from the opened apex (centre) and still escapes (right) as several of the team constrict the envelope, further to expel the air.

67

Club. This august and welcoming organisation, then 64 years old, had initially been proposed by a fivesome (three gentlemen and two ladies) when they were up in a balloon over the Crystal Palace. For our November assembly in 1965 there were, all around us, pictures of early aerial endeavour. The place looked most correct for a further initiation. Our 90 moderns rivalled their be-whiskered, top-hatted, plus-foured and straight-faced antecedents in enthusiasm and spirit, and did better still in cunning. Having deliberated and discussed they bounced the buck right back to me, before leaving merrily. 'Form a British Balloon and Airship Club,' they demanded; 'Oh yes, without delay.'

Those five who were airborne over the Crystal Palace could have had no idea how aviation would develop. The Aero Club which they proposed was subsequently founded on 4 September 1901. That was over two years before Orville and Wilbur Wright powered their flying machine above the ground of North Carolina. It was five years before any heavier-than-air machine flew in Europe (when Alberto Santos-Dumont coaxed his '14 bis' into the air). One year later a total of eight individuals had flown in Europe, briefly, insecurely, and erratically, causing many other individuals to argue that flight had no valid future. Lord Kelvin, brilliant in his field, had 'not the smallest molecule of faith in aerial navigation other than ballooning'. Thomas Edison, inventor of practically everything, reported earlier that 'the possibilities of the aeroplane ... have been exhausted'.

Both Wright brothers visited Europe in 1907, but did not bring their machine with them (and Wilbur had his first flight in a balloon). European journalism, suspicious of American claims to have preceded European efforts, headlined 'Flyers or Liars' and similar sentiments. Even when a Wright 'Flyer' arrived the following year there was still distrust. 'Le bluf continue,' wrote one Paris paper. When the plane had been uncrated, and had flown at Le Mans, Wilbur destroyed all opposition, once even remaining airborne, safely and well controlled, for two hours.

That famous event occurred seven years after the Royal Aero Club had been born. Its founders could not possibly have known (or even have guessed) that development of aviation would be so swift, so effective and so influential. As they floated over the Crystal Palace, no doubt busy with hampers and happy talk to the two young ladies also aloft, they may have been able to see the English Channel. They were visionaries in their way, but could not possibly have foreseen that a heavier-than-air machine

Flying in Switzerland can be exhilarating. Retrieve in Switzerland can be problematical.

would splutter its way across that same expanse of water a mere eight years later, prelude to its landing in a field by Dover.

It cannot be right to equate the development of ballooning in particular with that of aviation in general, but there are parallels. After that November meeting of 1965 I did initiate a club, did appoint a committee, did acquire a written constitution, and did arrange for a first meeting of paid-up (£2 a year) members to be held on August Bank Holiday 1966. Thirty-five of us then assembled in the social room of the London Gliding Club, Dunstable. It was a hasty and informal meeting, as almost all participants were engaged in aerial activities taking place on that 'Open Day', such as the inflation of four balloons. *Jambo* and an ex-RAF gas balloon were there, with Gerry Turnbull as the other pilot. We two gas-pilots took off in standard fashion, and I had a most enjoyable flight which ended by a memorable barbed-wire fence near Kineton in Warwickshire.

Back at the airfield there were two hot-air balloons, one fashioned to resemble the Montgolfier craft of 1783 and the other, a translucent thing of polythene and sticky tape, looking like no craft there had ever been. It split before take-off and, after a request for Sellotape from the attendant crowd, it was later pronounced fit for flight. It then flew with one man on board, but the Montgolfier flew on its own, together with great quantities of smoke exuding from its mouth. Unfortunately (such a key word in aerial endeavour) one of these devices contacted the gliding club's supply of electricity. The commentator had been commentating, but subsequent comments could only be guessed because instant silence overcame him. Nevertheless news soon spread that no more balloons – of any kind – would be allowed to fly.

It is an ill wind, they say, which blows no good. The gentle breeze which had sent those simple aerostats towards the wires was also ruffling the hair of a spectator named Don Cameron. 'Surely I can do better than that,' he muttered to himself (this being his favoured style of speech). A crucial seed was therefore sown. It soon received nourishment when Bill Williams, airship pilot of World War One, heard of Don's concern whether his employment as aeronautical engineer (with Hawker Siddeley) should be continued or given up to attend to aerostation. 'If work interferes with your hobby,' said the old man, still in love with l-t-a, 'you should give up work.'

Neither Bill, nor Don, nor any of us could have foreseen that, by the late 1990s, there would be 10,000 balloons around the world, a number having grown from a pathetic handful in the late 1960s. In that sense the founding of the Royal Aero Club and the subsequent founding of the British Balloon and Airship Club within its premises have paralleled each other. Millions of us now fly each year in aircraft. Several hundred thousand of us now fly annually by balloon. Who could have guessed either outcome? That fivesome over the Crystal Palace could not possibly have known, any more than I did when, stricken by conscience and a bulging file, inviting everyone 'who had expressed an interest in lighter-than-air' to attend that inaugural meeting little more than three decades ago.

No-one could have guessed that ballooning's rise would be quite so swift, the modern balloon starting its career several decades after Mickey Mouse did so.

CHAPTER 5

Mishaps and accidents

'So you're going ballooning, are you? Aren't you scared?... So you're going scuba-diving, are you? That should be fun.'
People in general are poor at assessing risk, whether for civil aircraft (big or small), step ladders, motoring, bus travel, scuba-diving – or flying by balloon.

AT ONCE THERE IS CONUNDRUM. No one wishes trouble (save perhaps for malevolent spectators) but the sport might have less appeal if entirely free of misadventure. Would cliff climbing create such devotion if, from time to time, someone did not fall? Would parachuting, pot-holing, car-racing, scuba-diving or other activities at which insurance men first raise their eyebrows (before they lift the premiums) be as attractive if occasional fatalities did not occur to boost appeal? However tranquil the sport of ballooning, with humans becoming gossamer – temporarily, does it too require some very harsh reality to interrupt its dream-like circumstance? If so it is interesting to wonder if an edge – of some sort – is crucial ingredient for human enterprise, such as starting commercial undertakings (when recommendation is contrary and funds are limited), such as disregarding advice (almost on principle) – and such as flying by lighter than air.

Don Cameron, whose company has made 5,500 balloons since it began (in his living room) almost 30 years ago, argues that balloons possess 'perceived danger'. Humans are not logical in assessing risks. They disregard step-ladders (which lead to dozens, or even hundreds, of deaths each year in Britain alone) and are alarmed by rabies (which kills two or three at most in huge endemic regions, like continental Europe or North America). Ballooning *seems* to be dangerous, with its wickerwork, its wind-borne passage, its soft material. Therefore, so runs this emotion, it *must be* dangerous.

People die in Britain from scuba-diving every year, but its image is of flippered feet paddling gently past underwater sights. Deaths from ballooning, per each airborne venture as against the waterborne of diving, are much less common, and yet ballooning causes greater apprehension.

'So you're going up in a balloon – aren't you scared?'

'So you're going scuba-diving – that should be fun.'

Cameron has acquired statistics concerning real ballooning hazard – as against the seeming kind. Chances of aerial death are:

1 per million flights with ordinary civil aircraft
27 per million flights with light aircraft
8 per million flights in gliders
4 per million flights in European balloons
11 per million flights in American balloons*

(*The greater danger within the United States is largely caused by the greater preponderance of above-ground electrical wiring.)

The actual apprehension in the air can also be wrong-headed, with the real danger assessed quite wrongly. Even for experienced pilots this can be true. Tom Sage, ballooning veteran, considers his most terrifying moment, scoring zero in its actual danger, was caused by the explosion of a crisps packet (this having expanded with increasing altitude). Its bang was terrifying, causing his heart – most understandably – to palpitate for the remainder of that day. Phil Dunnington, almost as long in ballooning years, hates being above 3,000 feet. Lower than that he is calm, content, relaxed, but the ground is more likely to be hurtful than mere height. (Indeed I once watched him, with face turned white then green as he vomited dislike – all too literally – of a swirling dust-devil twisting him wildly as it played at ground level with his balloon.)

There have been four ballooning fatalities within Britain since modern ballooning began. For the first two a ripping system opened at height, causing far too speedy a descent. The third involved one experienced individual, flying solo, who hit high-tension cables, either because he did not see them or he failed in his avoidance. Electricity also caused the fourth death after a balloon's collision with some wires near the Humber set alight the on-board propane. That basket's occupants either fell out or leaped out, several were badly burned (including the pilot) and the oldest – a woman – dying.

With a personal ballooning memory stretching back to 1961 it is, alas, easy to recall the deaths of other friends in other countries, but hard to think of factors linking them together. There was Barbara Keith who, in flying from Catalina Island to the Californian mainland (very early in hot air days), failed to reach the shore, as did almost all the others. Unfortunately, despite rescue boats detailed to follow each balloon, hers did not locate her until she had perished from prolonged immersion in the sea. Then came Francis Shields, ebullient house-builder from Philadelphia, who flew straight into an iron grille near the top of Vienna's telecommunications tower, together with two passengers. Malcolm Brighton, partner in many shared experiences, could not resist the invitation to pilot an ill-starred balloon with its two promoters from Long Island. They reached

It is hard thinking of factors which link ballooning accidents together, but they are always waiting to pounce, turning mishap into misery – or worse.

somewhere near Newfoundland before all three vanished utterly. Dick Wirth, balloon-creator and arch-competitor, was with others in a basket on the ground at Albuquerque when leaking propane caught alight. Some of them escaped but not Dick as he struggled to douse the fire. Ernst Krauer, a jovial Swiss who adored the Alps, flew too close one day, causing ice to sever ropes and killing all four on board.

If there is a common component it is well hidden, save that ill fortune chose those days to exert its influence. Why should only one of the Catalina racers not be found? Why should Francis hit that tower when three predecessors that afternoon had gone to the left or right of it? And why did Malcolm's flight have to end so tragically when other Atlantic hopefuls, preceding and succeeding that 1970 flight, were plucked to safety from the sea? As for Dick I suspect he could have saved himself by caring not a fig for others, and Ernst would be living still if he had loved the Alps, perhaps more wisely but less whole-heartedly. Maybe excessive courage was the common undoing of all such individuals. Charles Dollfus, premier French balloonist for half a century, emphasised the point after Francis Shields had taken so recklessly to the air: 'The fear of ballooning has been for me the best help throughout my long, varied and not-uneventful life as an aeronaut.' Fear can certainly be magnified by learning of experience elsewhere. A good day's ballooning, with clear skies, gentle breezes, sane company and soft landings, will boost confidence, putting the possibility of accident firmly to one side, but collecting accident reports, as I first did (in 1967) when chairing the international ballooning committee (of the FAI in Paris), can swiftly erode such ill-placed faith. As I took notes that year, with an increasingly anxious hand, I listed all seven which had occurred in the previous 12 months (a year, incidentally, when balloon flights were still scarce as the hot air renaissance had hardly begun). These were:

1 Balloon hit electric wires after landing. Caught fire. *(Germany)*
2 Partial explosion during deflation. *(Germany)*
3 Bad landing. Pilot broke both legs, and a passenger one foot. Another died from heart attack later. *(Germany)*
4 Balloon burst at 4,500 ft. No injuries as fabric provided sufficient parachuting effect. *(France)*
5 Balloon impaled on steeple while basket wedged on another steeple. Balloon destroyed. No injuries. *(France)*
6 Balloon landed in bushes. Torn to shreds by wind. *(France)*
7 Balloon hit 150 kV transmission line. Balloon destroyed. No injuries. *(France)*

Fortune can plainly be malevolent or extraordinarily beneficent. Francis, Dick, Ernst and Co. had suffered its darker side, but those who fail to undo a gas balloon's mouth before take-off, thereby causing the envelope to rupture, can ponder as they plummet downwards, at non-lethal speed, why they should be so blessed by fortune's fairer face. Fortune itself decides which face it wants to show.

Thirty years on from that FAI meeting I now read the 'accident and incident reports' gathered by the British Balloon and Airship Club. Once again I wonder at fortune's fickle ways, damaging here, relenting there, and forever playing fast and loose with people's happiness. It so happened there were six such reports in the latest gathering.

1 After a landing the balloon touched previously unseen 11 kV wires. Two of the eight basket wires severed. No injuries.
2 Both pilot lights failed, causing 'substantial contact' with trees. Envelope damaged. Firm landing. One twisted ankle.
3 Balloon struck power wires (seen only at last moment) on final approach. Electric cables parted, but only minor damage to balloon wiring.
4 Main burner inadvertently turned on, fortunately without its flame injuring anyone.
5 Balloon's crown line wrongly attached to tethering rope causing envelope deformation and sudden loss of lift when balloon at 100 ft.
6 A passenger misunderstood instructions, turning on a burner lever which caused superficial burns to two people, including the pilot, and to the envelope.

Electricity cables, sudden pilot light failure, burner ignition, sudden loss of lift at 100 ft – all had potential for disaster if fortune had chosen to smirk severely instead of smile reprimandingly. Only one twisted ankle and some superficial burns from that assortment! Not much, considering what there could have been, with death – as always – a fearful possibility. Charles Dollfus was right – it is good to be fearful. On the other hand it is also good to take risks, to chance your arm (as the saying goes), to try out novelty.

It looks wrong. It is wrong. There is all the difference in the world – and very suddenly – between a happy height of two feet and a lethal one of 20 feet.

Chancing your arm with electricity is not an option. All balloonists have electrical tales to tell, this aerial minefield being so critical. I, as timid as any when approaching electricity, once saw cable drums lying on the ground next to shiny pylons. Plainly their wiring was not yet attached, a fact all the plainer as we drew nearer. There was nothing but air between each upright structure. 'Bet you can't fly between the pylons,' shouted a fellow balloonist, flying within hailing distance. And he was right. I could not bring myself to do so. Nor, as it happened, could he.

Pylons – and the wires between them – cause more ballooning accidents than any single other entity. Such encounters usually have unhappy endings – with severed wires, sparks, fire, and high voltages an unpleasant mixture – but, occasionally, there can be (something of) a lighter side. An Englishman, flying over Lancashire, became suddenly enshrouded, an instant mist trimming visibility to nothing of value. The ground had gone. The sky had gone. So a landing was most necessary. Unfortunately, no sooner were some wires observed than they were ensnaring that balloon. Flashes testified to their 400 kV liveliness, with 'brilliant electric blue sparks in all directions,' as the pilot later reported. One way and another, with lines melting and gravity asserting its authority, the basket and its occupants were lowered heavily to the ground. There were broken bones, and burned skin, but all were still alive. The pilot therefore requested assistance, using the emergency frequency of 121.5.

'Hi there Buddy, what seems to be the problem?' queried a Delta Airlines pilot circling 6,000 feet above O'Hare Airport, Chicago. England's balloonist, dumfounded by quirks of radio but delighted to be heard, started to explain. 'The problem was not in telling him that we were a balloon in distress, but that we were in Rossendale, Lancashire, *England*.' A second Mayday call got a reply from nearer home, from *Speedbird 190* leaving Heathrow. Very soon help was on its way, and all that basket's occupants were speedily helicoptered to hospital in nearby Manchester.

In Brazil, when electricity is involved (or likely to be so), they have been known to do things even speedier. On a blustery day in 1997, with balloons near Iguaçu heading for some high voltage, the manager of a forewarned power station shut down all current to those wires.

The cat's-cradle of electric wiring strung over the countryside is the biggest single peril for balloonists, and always to be feared.

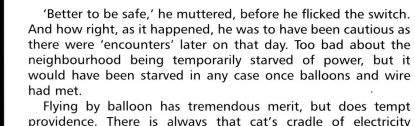

'Better to be safe,' he muttered, before he flicked the switch. And how right, as it happened, he was to have been cautious as there were 'encounters' later on that day. Too bad about the neighbourhood being temporarily starved of power, but it would have been starved in any case once balloons and wire had met.

Flying by balloon has tremendous merit, but does tempt providence. There is always that cat's cradle of electricity waiting to ensnare. There is propane, or hydrogen, and they both catch fire. Above all there is altitude, and the hard and solid ground waiting down below. Mishaps will presumably always occur, and so will accidents. Such outcomes will never vanish, but these disturbing thoughts can be quietly shelved – for now. Let this section on misadventure therefore be concluded with a happy incident (which should never have occurred). It did give fate great opportunity for mishap, but it never came to pass.

'Do you want the good news first, or the bad?' crackled the radio shortly after a friend and I had taken off near Naivasha in Kenya. We opted for the bad and it swiftly came our way.

'Well, it's 4.30 in the morning, and it'll be dark for the next couple of hours.'

It would be a poor couple of balloonists who did not already know it was dark. It would also be a hapless pair who did not know the time, whether of day or night, but that – in brief – was our predicament. We had planned on an early take-off, the better to see a bright new dawn, but had been more than a touch premature. In fact we were about to see – if that is the word – an awful lot of night.

Minor mishap or accident-in-waiting? Only time would tell. As nights go – and this one had much time to go – it seemed blacker than most. Even when we could detect – or thought we had detected – the outline of some distant hill-top a fresh and necessary squirt from the burner would blind even our imagination. So we tried covering our eyes when burning, and opening them when only the pilot light was active, a procedure causing us to see virtually nothing for 100 per cent of the time. What we ought to have been able to observe, even at night in that volcanic, escarpmented, and generally unnerving portion of East Africa's rift valley, was something of its most distinctive horizon, with some bits several thousand feet higher than some other bits. As it was, blinded by the burner or blind behind our

'It would be a poor couple of balloonists who did not already know it was dark.' It would indeed, but there were reasons – of a sort.

hands, we settled for seeing nothing. The occasion was therefore rich with possibilities, most involving abrupt encounters with steep-sided hunks of rock.

'Oh yes, what was the good news?' we suddenly remembered and then transmitted.

Back at the take-off site they had calculated that we on board had just sufficient fuel to take us into daylight, that's if we were economical, did not fly too high, were extremely lucky, and were not heading for Longonot, the local peak at 9,100 ft. As an example of comforting news we had heard better on occasions in the past, but the past was all irrelevant as we stood there, being economical, not climbing much, hoping Longonot was elsewhere, longing for good luck, and wondering how we had got into such a mess.

The fault lay in the many early starts on previous days. Africa is best for ballooning when at its least African, before the sun is burning into another day, before thermals have given pelicans and vultures an easy time for flight. In short, flight is best at each day's earliest. Consequently we had become used to tumbling out of bed in darkness, drinking coffee as gentle dawn crept into the silent sky, inflating our balloon in twilight, and then taking off to travel within the softness of that early hour.

The unhappy fact – one day – that our alarm-caller had mis-read his watch, had shouted at us all, had brought water to the boil, and had poured coffee into mugs before helping in the pre-flight tasks had been the basic fault. While we were all stumbling upon, tripping over, bumping into and inflating our balloon not one of us had bothered to inspect our individual time-pieces when busily checking rip lines, and propane, and generally making ready for the pre-dawn experience which had been planned. We had wanted to be up there before the day arrived. The fact that we had carelessly caused a pre-pre-dawn experience could therefore be attributed to many early starts, and to a group of individuals each assuming that others knew what they were doing better than himself. This resulted in an even more fundamental fact (of dominant interest to the two on board). Everyone had been at fault, but only two of us had ended up in the firing line.

It was very dark up there. We could see no land, no lights, no sheens of water from nearby lakes. For altitude we compromised at 10,000 feet, this being just higher than

To be afloat over every form of man-made thing, and to be above ground-based restriction, can induce a most pleasurable form of arrogance.

Longonot's volcanic peak and 5,000 feet above most ground in that area. To have flown higher would have consumed more fuel, and we wished to be economical because the prospect of a landing in the dark did not have much appeal. In fact little did appeal at that early hour, with nothing to see – except in our mind's eye which repeatedly envisioned cliff contact, rocky tragedy, maiming and mayhem. We searched and searched for something in all that ink, but nothing was there, nothing whatsoever. Then, tremendously close at hand, were the two of us when another burner squirt suddenly illuminated our basket home, our lonely isolation in a world of black.

W hat, we kept on wondering, might occur? Would the occasion be no more than a mishap, an event to recall over pints of beer, or were we experiencing a slow build-up to fatality? The burner's blindings prevented us from seeing gauges (difficult to read at the best of times) and our fuel's endurance could not therefore be assessed. Besides, when would darkness finally yield? When would there be light enough to distinguish solid rock from wild imaginings? And when would we learn what fate, presumably prescient in its planning, had up its sleeve in store for us? For the present we each could only stand, watch the dark (if that makes sense), wonder why our companion looked quite so glum, and wait and wait for dawn.

It comes, so they say, from the East, but where on Earth was that? We had no compass and therefore no idea, but it would come no faster whether or not we knew where best to look. In the end, like everything suddenly conspicuous, we were surrounded by the light of dawn long after it appeared. (That dazzling burner flame had much to answer for.) Maybe the sun does rise in the East but, before the solar globe itself appears, its light is everywhere, West as much as East, and North as well as South. We learned that truth while still having no idea where East might be, but that was no longer of concern. The darkness had been taken from our eyes, and we could see once more.

Not much, admittedly, but there were outlines in the sky. The land beneath was still a mystery, but every time we looked at it the shapes below were clearer, better, sharper than they had been a minute earlier. We had no idea what might arise, having no idea either where we were or had been in the dark. Therefore we were as aliens, knowing which planet was below but knowing little more. Gradually there were valleys, still a little misty, and hills at comfortable distances, but there was no sign of people, not a home, not a road, not a thing save bewildering landscape for miles and miles and miles. Rather more importantly we still had fuel to spare.

So it was a mishap after all. We could now see the cliffs and rocks. We would land at our convenience, even if we had absolutely no idea of our location. There is still much of Africa as it used to be, and we floated over its pristine land entranced, delighted and regularly charmed. The mind's eye visions, with injury and death, were now quite laughable, and we giggled at each other in renewed delight. As for retrieval that was the problem of those who had launched us prematurely. We would fly until the fuel was virtually exhausted. Then, as the wind was gentle, we would touch down but keep the envelope inflated. It would serve as beacon for as long as there was propane to keep it buoyant. Then it would die around us, and we would drape it over bushes to act as guidance.

And that was how the day did end, not crashing blindly into cliff but sinking softly on to ground. The event had become a tale for telling, perhaps over pints of beer. The fine line between horror and happiness had been seen most clearly, and we had ended on its merry side. That is the trouble with misadventure. Humans are pawns, doing their best but not every time succeeding. There is conundrum all along, and there is luck, with mishap and accident part and parcel of the scene. That fact, however much we may deny it, possibly adds to the allure. Would we like ballooning quite so much if, every now and then, there were not some accident? It gives the sport an edge, a brink, an admission of recklessness, however careful we may try to be in avoiding all mistakes.

'You're going ballooning, are you? So aren't you scared?'

In earlier and pioneering years, before flexi-rigid poles separated burner frames from baskets, a landing could be damaging to pioneer craniums.

CHAPTER 6

The soloists

Ballooning is a gregarious business, with fellow passengers enjoying a shared experience. There are also individualists, happy to be solo, ready to leave the crowd behind, and feeling (so they say) like birds – however distant the resemblance.

A BALLOON NEEDS CALM WEATHER IN WHICH TO FLY. A balloon also needs open or undeveloped areas in which to land. And a balloon ride is a gregarious occasion, with a few friends within each basket to enjoy the shared experience. No wonder, therefore, that windy Britain is more beset by balloonists than any other nation. No wonder that well-developed Britain, with intensive agriculture and intensive use of every kind, sees more balloon landings per square mile than anywhere else. And also no wonder, bearing similar logic in mind, that the United Kingdom is lead country for one-man balloons, for doing it on your own, for leaving all togetherness and conviviality back there on the ground.

More amazing still is the further fact that these individualists, these one-man bands and solo invaders of the sky, do actually like to congregate (but not on board their own contrivances). The year 1997 witnessed the 15th successive annual get-together of people who like flying apart from each other. Known as One Mans' Meets they are plainly meat for some and not for ordinary balloonists who prefer to travel with other people, to take up friends, to be mutually involved. Nevertheless the one-manners are as competitive as any. They do wish to win – on their own. They do assemble – before departing single-handedly. And then – may the best one-man win.

Phil Dunnington, formerly with conventional aviation before his hobby took him to Camerons, has been prime mover in this direction. He admits the one-manners are best in calm conditions, but the crowds love them, so he says, for their apparent recklessness. Solo balloonists, being the aerostatic equivalent of daring young men on the flying trapeze, are much appreciated. The sight of legs dangling from very little of a seating arrangement, this suspended beneath a burner smaller than most and a relatively minute envelope, can seem for observers to be nearer their vision of flying through the air with the greatest of ease than the normal upright basket-load.

If the crowds could see the landings of such one-manners they might be even more delighted. Instead of touching down toes first, and then tipping face downwards, the one-men prefer landing backwards and heel first, thereby giving their bodies a less damaging time, even if those same bodies did not actually see where they were going. To some extent these one-man aerostats are a form of reversion to the very first propane balloon. Ed Yost, then test pilot (of Raven Industries), flew on

There can be no simpler way of becoming airborne than acquiring a diminutive envelope, filling it with heat, sitting on not much of a chair, and then ascending in the sky.

not much of a camping stool and with hardly any extraneous equipment to keep him company. His first envelope was only 30,000 cubic feet. The modern varieties no longer qualify as genuine one-person balloons (for the one-man meets) if larger than 42,000 cubic feet, and Ed's would therefore qualify.

Thunder & Colt, balloon manufacturers, built the first so-called Cloud Hopper, and have continued to make and amend it. Encouragement to do so came from the film *Green Ice*. Its script called for three men to fly from the top of a 500-ft Mexican skyscraper, and to do so beneath three one-man balloons, each of 14,000 cubic feet. It was surely unnerving to inflate, ascend

and suddenly be confronted by considerable altitude. Looking down the side of a tall building can induce vertigo and unease very readily. Actually to fly over such an edge, with nothing but concrete, cars and lesser construction well below, must be nightmarish, and the pilots involved (Robin Batchelor, Colin Prescot, Ian Ashpole, Graham Elson) remember the filming, and its fears, most acutely. Making everything worse (such as palpitations) was insistence by the film-men that all three balloons should be tied together *and* attached to the skyscraper for retrieval should additional filming and repeat departures be necessary.

Thunder & Colt had made one previous Cloudhopper (for Smirnoff) but the six constructed for Mexico helped to promote this form of flying. The company still makes such small balloons, and their latest Cloudhopper version comes in three sizes, 21,000, 25,000 and 31,000 cubic feet. The inflated diameters are therefore 10.9, 11.4, and 15.6 metres. Their envelopes weigh 36, 40 and 50 kilograms, and maximum all-up weight (balloon + fuel + pilot) is 210, 250 and 310 kilograms respectively. As for the weight of everything (which is *not* fuel, pilot or envelope) that is a mere 16.2 kg, or 36 lb. When properly packed for transport the device measures 43 by 16 by 15 inches. Its extra of a propane tank can be any normal variety containing from 40 to 80 litres.

Brian Boland, of Vermont, has specialised in building light-weight balloons, his latest being a 41,000 cubic footer which is a masterpiece of miniaturisation. The basket (wholly inappropriate as a term) is a few rods, some cross-bracing wires, and a base which can all be folded into a most convenient package. The propane cylinder is constructed in two halves, and its internal space is therefore available for anything else, such as clothes and personal gear when not occupied by propane. This whole device can therefore travel on aircraft as personal baggage. How extraordinary it is that an entire flying machine can be carried by a single individual, and be smaller than conventional suitcases which many people consider crucial accompaniment for shirts, socks, toothbrushes and the like.

One-man showmanship has been extended beyond dangling legs and waving arms. For instance, they can be – and have been – 'stacked'. Several can be so positioned, providing the wind is modest and kind, one above the other, with each pilot temporarily attached to the crown of the balloon below him.

Occasionally the one-manners will assemble at 'one-man meets' or other gatherings, and even talk, before disappearing – singly – as is their variegated custom.

The sight is therefore the airborne equivalent of that circus routine when humans stand upon each other's shoulders to form a pyramid.

As for the pilots of cloudhoppers, sky chariots and the like they have no need for stunts to gain their pleasure. The fact of sitting there, map on lap, one hand on the throttle, and nothing but air between feet and ground is more bird-like, so they say, than anything else. They are kestrels, hovering while looking for a meal. They are pelicans or eagles, with wings outstretched, maintaining altitude in effortless style. They are one-manners, enjoying the solitude, and revelling in such a singular experience. (There are also two-person versions, further variants on the theme, for twosomes who wish to fly that way.)

The one-man advertising matter proclaims the benefits. 'Enjoy flight without restrictions of space and vision imposed by the walls of a basket... add a new dimension to the sponsor's promotions... appreciate armchair comfort (as) you get a well padded seat, padded armrests, padded uprights, map bag, radio mount, footrest, easily accessible controls...'. Some contrary (and perhaps more normal) people quite like the restrictions imposed by a basket's walls. With increasing altitude they can wish the walls were higher still. Such people do not mind leaning on a basket's rim, or moving position, or having agreeable companions conveniently close to hand (or encircling arm). They will probably stick to ordinary baskets, happy with the conviviality – and delighted that the wickerwork restriction prevents them from falling overboard.

Britain *is* a windy place, Britain *is* developed, and ballooning *is* a gregarious affair. No wonder then, to repeat the initial message, that Britain is crowded with balloonists, is beset by landing problems, and some of Britain's pilots like nothing more than to be on their own, unrestricted, adding new dimension, and sitting in a chair which lands backwards when that time arrives. There is then no need even for retrieve. Just pick up the balloon – and walk.

'Enjoy flight without restriction... add a new dimension... appreciate armchair comfort...' Chateau d'Oex, Switzerland.

CHAPTER 7

Special shapes

For their first 193 years, almost every balloon was conventionally shaped, with a bulbous top, a gradual tapering down below, and a basket (of sorts) at the base. In consequence everyone knew what a balloon looked like – but then came 1976…

CERTAIN OBJECTS HAVE APPROPRIATED a shape entirely for themselves. Pears are indisputably pear-shaped. If anything else, such as a light bulb, is somewhat similar it is said to be pear-shaped. The pear got there first and is entitled to prior claim. So too with bananas being banana-shaped (save that nothing else has ever wished to mimic that peculiar design). Hour-glasses are hour-glass-shaped, with women – allegedly – hour-glass-shaped at the start of the 20th century (although a case could be made for hour-glasses being women-shaped as women got there first). Corkscrews are corkscrew-shaped, bottles are bottle-shaped, mugs are mug-shaped, and on and on with – somewhere in the lengthy list – balloons being balloon-shaped. Of course they are, being fattest at the top and lessening nearer the bottom, unless they too should be classified as another pear-shaped shape.

The very first balloon pair to become airborne, although differing in their lifting mediums, were sufficiently similar to give birth to a multitude of objects exploiting their motif. There was a round bit at the top, a narrowing of sorts, and then a car/gondola/nacelle/capsule/basket somewhere down below. Door-handles, mirrors, hair-brushes, spoons, lamps, walking-stick tops, pictures, lavatory chain pulls, clothes hooks – you name it, you got it, particularly during the 18th century when balloons were all the rage, the style, the *dernier cri* (or even the first cry when balloons were *à la mode*). Everyone suddenly knew what a balloon looked like. It was balloon-shaped, and it continued to be balloon-shaped for years and years to come.

Until 1976. In that year *Golly* (registration G-OLLI) took to the air. By modern yardsticks this new flying thing was almost conventional, being little more than a standard balloon at the top (black with two eyes to resemble a face) and blue, yellow and red below mimicking the body of Robertsons Jams famous Afro-emblem. At the very base of this novel aerostat was a basket plus its burner, the flame of which pointed directly up the trouser legs. Total volume was 31,000 cubic feet, just sufficient to take one pilot through the sky, and this new shape, with its sideways-looking eyes, caused other eyes to look and question more directly. Why did balloons have to be balloon-shaped? What about, say, light-bulb-shaped or, a touch less round, spark-plug-shaped?

With a little ingenuity (or, at times, a lot) almost every earth-bound shape can be turned into a balloon which then flies into the air.

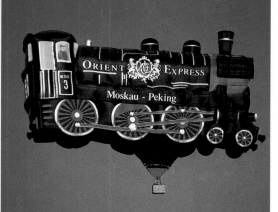

Golly (main picture) and a handful of Golly's lineal descendants. Somewhere at the base of each and every one is a basket, a burner and a pilot controlling these most improbable aircraft. Is there any shape, from Sonic Hedgehogs to Orient Expresses, from motorbikes to cows to elephants to dinosaurs, which cannot be cunningly transformed into yet another balloon?

Very soon a plug, a bulb and other objects were flying through the sky, or rather flying through it before, on occasion, hurtling to the ground. The sparking plug balloon was tall and thin – as befits a sparking plug. Many of us, excitedly watching its ascent at Cirencester, were suddenly – no less excitedly – watching its descent. Plainly, as we realised instantaneously, there was much to be said for the bulbous form of a conventional balloon, its rotundity thrusting through the air without deformity. The plug's tallness and thinness meant, as the thing ascended, that its top bent over, thus reducing the internal volume (due to constriction at the bend) and simultaneously preventing burner-heated air from reaching the top half (after this was pointing sideways or even downwards). With its volume and its temperature both reduced the plug-balloon was bound to fall. Fortunately that very descent caused the bent-over section to flip upright again, thus returning internal volume to normal and permitting an inrush of hot air. There was aerial inrush on the ground as well when we, anxious spectators every one, began to breathe again. We knew the making of special shapes could be difficult, but had learned their flying could also have its tricks.

Some of the novel forms, cleverly made and then skilfully manoeuvred through the sky, possessed characteristics which even clever manufacturers and cunning pilots did not foresee. The pipe (G-PIPE), for example, had a bowl more or less balloon-shaped, and also a stem pointing upwards from that bowl's base. At each inflation this thin, long thing would initially be lying in desultory fashion along the ground. Then, the bowl becoming complete and hot air seeking further areas to fill, this stem would begin to stiffen as it assumed its proper shape. From flaccidity to erection – medical terms engagingly appropriate – this process of engorgement was received with happy approbation by every man and every woman of every waiting crowd. That pipe of a balloon was much favoured among the special shapes, not least for the triumph of its consummation mere moments before, with sufficient rigidity, it managed to leave the ground.

Hofmeister's bear was another whose character, and therefore popularity, seemed greater than had been planned. During its television commercials the bear would walk with a swagger, a two-footed, street-wise, know-it-all and grandilo-

'A pair of jeans helped to spread the popularity of special shapes... this second non-balloon-shape balloon to be constructed.' Action Man is nearer Number 300 in the odd-shape production line.

quent air. Its shoulders (or rather those of the man within its suit) moved haughtily, arrogantly, and high-handedly, making this the *grand seigneur* of bears. So too, most amazingly, when the same trade-mark was hundreds of times larger and flying up aloft. Its arms, even when fully inflated with hot air, were never totally stiff. Instead they oscillated with a panache mimicking the television bear. The colossal air-filled shoulders swaggered in equal style, and the imperious airborne animal was as engagingly superior in style and general demeanour as its filmed (and human) counterpart. The airborne thing, so perfect in its impersonation, was therefore – and most entrancingly – a joy to watch, particularly when it chose to fly alongside as swaggering companion above the English countryside.

So what have action men, airliners, apples, Arabs, babies, bananas, batteries, beer mugs, boats, books, bottles, bowler-hatted men, boxes, cacti, cakes, candies, carrots, cars, castles, cigarette packs, clowns, coffee pots, composers, computers, cows, crescent moons, dinosaurs, disk jockeys, dogs, Donald ducks, dolls, dragons, drink cans, eagles, eggs, elephants, encyclopaedias, film cassettes, fire extinguishers, flower pots, flying saucers, fork-lift trucks, foxes, golf balls, hamburgers, hares, heads, horses, hot-dogs, houses, ice-cream cones, koalas, kookaburras, lions, liquorice allsorts, marshmallows, Michelin men, Mickey mice, mobile phones, motorbikes, newspapers, oil cans, oranges, parcels, parrots, peacocks, peanuts, pears, petrol pumps, pigs, piggy banks, polar bears, propane tanks, pylons, rabbits, raspberries, Russian dolls, salamis, shoes, Sonic hedgehogs, space shuttles, sphinxes, stoves, strawberries, tigers, toilet rolls, tractors, trains, trolleys, trucks, vans, watches, wheels, windmills, witches, and Uncle Tom Cobbleighs got to do with each other? Not much, save that they all (bar Uncle Tom) have been made into balloons.

Somewhere down at the bottom of each and every one of these has been a basket, a burner and a pilot. They do fly, and it is always very weird when, suspended from a conventional aerostat and watching the world go by, a gigantic motorcycle (or house or train or car) floats suddenly into view. One's own balloon, excitingly coloured but conventionally shaped, can abruptly seem tedious, old hat, and wretchedly commonplace when surrounded by exotica on every hand, when Beethoven passes by, expressionless and stone deaf, when a four-pack of beer cans is just beyond his reach, and when *Tyrannosaurus Rex*

Suddenly one's own balloon, flamboyantly coloured and excitingly designed, can seem old hat, tedious, even boring, when a polar bear or dragon emerges next in line.

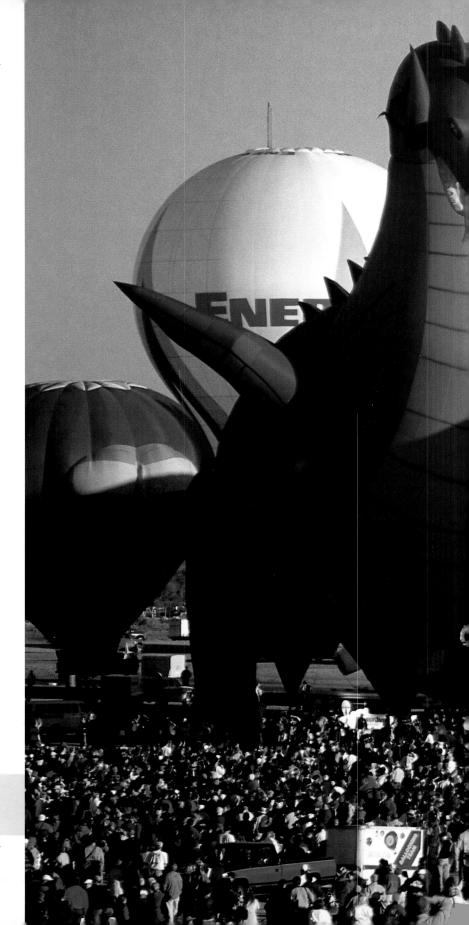

looks more than capable of eating everything in sight. The terrifying carnivore should start with Rupert Bear, still wearing his outfit of red scarf, check trousers and expressionless face as he has done since beginning cartoon life so many years ago.

A pair of jeans helped to spread the popularity of special shapes, as well as assisting manufacturers in their special skill. The jeans (second non-balloon-shape balloon to be constructed) were given the proper shape as worn. They were therefore waist-wide and waist-round at their apex. Their two legs were correctly positioned down below, initially with openings at the base of each. These, on a trial flight, then sagged in an unsatisfactory manner. Only when when one leg-end was sealed in a rounded form, and when all hot air entered via the other, did they look as jeans should look, albeit 100 feet high and floating through the air.

Normal balloons take on their created shape without difficulty. Special shapes need ingested air to fill every awkward (and designed) space, a statement easier to make than to arrange. The feet of polar bears must look correct; so too the claws of birds, the legs of dogs, the handles of mugs and cans. Therefore it is not only amazing when a motorbike flies by to provide aerial company. It is also intriguing to wonder just how air has been arranged to meet every portion of its frame, and how its air in general stays warm enough to provide the necessary lift. All the houses, trains, trucks and so on are each individual miracles.

Packing them up is a different kind of miracle. Even traditional balloons pose problems, caused by retained air, when the time comes for coercing all their fabric within a bag. A special shape, with feet, noses, claws, arms, handles and all manner of protrusions, can take much longer – very much longer – before all the air is finally expelled. There are holes which can be opened, and various vents, but the packing of a special shape is often accompanied by the sight of friends, of alleged friends, hurrying elsewhere for some lesser task. Special shapes have their special problems, in their inflation, in their flying, and in their diminution, but their appeal is also special and always worth the effort – on someone else's part.

Advertisers have had much to do with the promotion of novel shapes, always happy to see crowds gazing fondly at a tremendous version of their company's product flying through the air. There must be shapes which have not yet been used, but they do not readily come to mind.

A major spur to all this special endeavour came from a single individual. He was very rich. He was, in major part, a showman. He adored balloons as well as travelling, and had once ballooned, in piecemeal fashion, across the United States. Never shy in proclaiming capitalism, the system which had done him proud, he was Malcolm Forbes, owner of *Forbes Magazine* and of much else, such as a huge chateau in Normandy. From behind this enormous dwelling, to which he had invited – as frequently – a great quantity of guests, a duplicate suddenly arose one day, another Chateau de Balleroy, this tremendous novelty then ascending to fly above the original. Showman, wealth, ballooning and fun had been happily coalesced. The new structure was none other than a special shape, a hot air balloon with basket, burner and pilot below its windowed, turreted, and chateau-form to keep it all in trim.

Of course, with money, energy and enthusiasm forever flowing from this much-loved individual, he did not stop at a mere chateau. The motorbike was also his idea, as yet another of his enthusiasms took on this novel form. So too a sphinx, for he was involved with Egypt at the time. Then a Fabergé egg (for he had bought one), the Minar of Pakistan (because he was going there) and an elephant and a Kyoto shrine (solely because he was off to visit Thailand and Japan). 'If I'm flying beneath a golden temple it must be Japan ...'. Next came Suleiman the Magnificent, yet more magnificent than the others (and easier to control, being more upright and much less horizontal). There was also, somewhat inevitably, a fattened *Forbes Magazine* flying through the sky.

His final request, despatched as with the others to Cameron Balloons, was for a macaw. This was planned to have its maiden voyage, most appropriately in Brazil, and did look resplendent, being superbly coloured as befits this most excellent of tropical birds. Then news came through, with the macaw all ready to fly, that its eccentric and buoyant purchaser had died most suddenly. They were sad, at Camerons, that such a friend had gone, but also a touch relieved – it is easy to suspect – that yet another difficult or well-nigh impossible request (there had been 11 in all) would come their way from a client for whom difficult or well-nigh impossible requests had formed a way of life.

Malcolm Forbes was a particular case, but not entirely on his own. A recent request was for a Scotsman. He was to be fully

They look astonishing when on the ground. They seem even more bizarre when in the air and when some extravagance arrives to keep one company.

equipped with all the kit that Scotsmen (sometimes) wear, namely – from the bottom up – shoes, spats, stockings, knees, kilt, sporran, jacket, buttons, cape, bagpipe, worried frown, puffed cheeks, and glengarry at the crown. The pipes would, if possible, make their specific sound – somehow, this noise being optimum when about one mile away. And that is how this extraordinary addition to the list of special shapes ascended in the air. He did look terrific. He also even sounded good, the noise escaping from a loudspeaker within the basket, this rectangle of wickerwork suspended, with a view above it prized by some, straight beneath the kilt.

Human brilliance lies behind the creation of all these outstanding airborne shapes, but computer brilliance and machine-cutting brilliance are also crucial. Anyone who has ever cut out curtains or even cushion-covers will know how easy it is to be left with cut-off sections, too small, too wrongly-coloured or wrongly-shaped to be used elsewhere. A cunning computer will do better, leaving next to no material. Similarly a cunning machine can run over fabric effortlessly, not troubled by all the ins and outs and cutting perfectly. A special-shaped balloon is itself an accumulation of scores of special shapes, of fabric, of colour, of size. The clever humans do need clever contrivances to help them do their job.

Most of the thrust for the creation of special shapes – apart from the wishes of unique individuals – comes from the advertising world. For a logo or a product to fly through the air, particularly over crowds, has proved irresistible for many an advertising manager. Flying Pictures, the British organisation with more shapes to promote than any other, started 20 years ago as the Hot Air Balloon Company. It began when an advertising man, Colin Prescot, and a ballooning man, Robin Batchelor, met – as it happened – in a pub. The initial name changed as the firm expanded beyond balloons, but balloons are still a mainstay.

The earliest client was Terry's, chocolate manufacturers, who saw advantage in aerial promotion, and many big names since then – Budweiser, Unipart, Sainsbury, and Agfa, for example – have been enthusiastic for this form of display. Turnover has now reached £4.5 million, an astonishment for anyone still thinking that balloons are anachronistic oddities, hangovers from Edwardian times, fit only for merriment or jest when they fly to join the sky. The special shapes *are* odd, and *do* look out of place, but that only heartens advertising managers. They

'Someone must have fallen out,' cried anxious onlookers, and with ample reason for their anxiety when Festo floated by.

know that people *do* look, and they tend to look with a smile upon their faces. Those smiles sell products, so they say, and that is why it pays to advertise, even in the sky.

There is also a special shape airship. The shape is not especially special, being not much more than a large nose projecting from the face of a round airship. Instead it is the thing's spherical configuration which is so remarkable. This has no rudders or fins, and its directional control is achieved by varying and deflecting thrust from two engines attached to the envelope. The novelty was created by Swedish-born Hakan Colting, the man behind Colting Balloons (of 1975) and also the latter part of Thunder & Colt (which later, in its complex history, was bought by Cameron Balloons). Colting now lives in Canada and, by taking his rotund device above Ontario to 7,450 feet, promptly broke nine world records (for classes BA2 to BA10).

Perhaps the very best ideas are always the very simplest. Once upon a time balloons were all balloon-shaped, but they have subsequently been fashioned into (seemingly) every other form, beginning with G-OLLI, passing through 300 others, and still far from ending. Suddenly, as complete reversal, a balloon has been fashioned which imitates, not motor cars or beer cans, not mythic monsters or real animals, but a balloon, save that it is upside-down. The ordinary balloon outline, so well known, so indentifiable, so much a bulge at the top and a tapering below, has been turned upon its head. For many this amazing innovation (dreamed up by ballooning man Nick Purvis) is the favoured special shape of all. It looks so perfectly ridiculous, with its mock basket at the top, and its tapering lower down *above* its greatest bulk which is nearest to the base. It is quite superb.

Allegedly, with these stories easy to believe, ground-based onlookers, aware of a terrible travesty, have telephoned authorities with desperate news.

'A balloon is the wrong way up,' they say; 'The people must have fallen out because the basket's at the top.'

An ambulance was even waiting for all injured parties (or mere bodies) when the upside-downer came to rest near Bristol after the maiden voyage. Best of all is when this Festo balloon (named for a power-press company) flies with a partner, an identical balloon (as near as dammit) save that it looks – and is – the right way up. A brilliant idea! Simple and eye-catching, fun and effective (so much so that two more upside-downers have been ordered plus another five conventionals). The wheel of

special shapes has therefore turned full circle. For many observers the most amazing shape of all is now the one which began it all, the balloon shape, except that on this particular occasion it is made to fly – and look – as if it is upside-down.

In short, balloons are still balloon-shaped, save for all those others which are not.

CHAPTER 8

Competition flying

'**A**s the golfer said, "The more I practice, the luckier I get." So too with ballooning. There is skill in bending chance towards a desirable end, in giving Dame Fortune a push in the right direction, in blending human cunning with opportunity.'

'SO HOW'S IT GOING?'

'Well, I scored a 1.00 metre on a fly-on, Ian did a 12.80 drop on a very fast PDG, and Dave mistook a road for the grid line on his hesitation waltz. Right now it's what you call so-so.'

'Thanks, I'll see you at the elbow.'

Worse still, for those at a loss, the talk may be the first conversation in English (for that is what it is) to be overheard during the previous hour. Similar chat will also have been proceeding, in Japanese or German, Hungarian or Australian, leaving casual onlookers (and overhearers) not much more ignorant while stepping past the familiar trappings of inflation fans at full buzz, of crown lines tautening, of burners burning, and aeronauts about to aeronaut.

'Das Elbow wahr furchtbar. Viel besser ist ein PDG.'

'Hol van a W.C.? Beszel angolul vagy franciaul?'

'Give me a Watership Down over a Gordon Bennett any day.'

It might as well be in Greek for the uninitiated. It possibly *is* Greek if the event is international, but it is meat and drink for all who love competition flying, with its amalgam of pilot declared goals, of judge declared goals, and of goals thought up by imaginative competition directors one hour earlier.

Balloons, as everyone knows, can only travel with the wind. The wind, as everyone also knows, blows as it chooses, with no one able to modify its direction. Therefore the notion of competitive ballooning seems strangled at birth, with every participant being subject to the same overwhelming forces of the encircling atmosphere. The fact that competitions *are* held, and that balloonists *do* compete, is due partly to the human urge for confronting others (and hoping to win) but also because the winds are inconsistent.

This human compulsion is very strong. It can start (in some) the moment they claim that 'mine is better than yours'. Sticks are thrown to float downstream. Gobstoppers and conkers are made to last. Stones are lobbed, further, higher, faster. Falling leaves are caught. Cans are knocked from pedestals. Computer enemies are zapped. Speed is extracted from carts with wheels, from bikes, from anything which moves. And then, when childhood has – as is alleged – been left behind, the rivalry persists. It becomes the all-absorbing sport of gaining directional control with huge hot air balloons.

Wind is as variable as the assortment of individuals who like to use it. There are some general rules (as there are with humans). In theory, and in the northern hemisphere, winds

To fly low means going slow – usually, and this means being close to ground-based things – most certainly.

blow about 30 degrees further to the right at 3,000 feet than when near the ground. In practise, along with contrary humans, they can fail to obey this general law. There is always a basic wind direction on any given day, but that is adjustable by seemingly everything lying in its path. Air currents will not, of course, go through brick walls (or houses or factories) and will also take the easy way around a wood. They flow faster over hills, being compressed by the rising land, and then relax, or even curl over, on each hill's other side. Warmer ground, such as dry cornfield, will heat the air passing up above, causing that warm air to rise. Cooler ground, such as any lake, has the opposite effect, leading every new balloonist to wonder why intended level flight has become yo-yo-like instead. Even when identical balloons are launched in identical style from an identical location they soon diverge, some going higher, and some to left or right of the average passage through the air.

Hence the ability for humans to compete, to take advantage of all these vagaries. It can seem like chance, when similar balloons are launched in similar style, which one goes left and which goes right, but competitors do not like that word. They admit luck is relevant, and often crucial, but it is not the total influence. As the golfer said, 'The more I practise, the luckier I get'. So too with ballooning. There is skill in bending chance towards a desirable end, in giving Dame Fortune a push in the right direction, in blending human cunning with opportunity.

Besides, unlike a lottery's random choice of winners, the same ballooning names do tend to be proclaimed at prize-giving time. Pilots doing better than the rest on one occasion are more likely to do well next time. It can seem unfair, as we used to yell when our conker burst apart, or when our stick arrived last from beneath the bridge, but we soon learned of conkers steeped in vinegar, of the one water current proving fastest every time, and we honed our skills accordingly.

'It's unfair,' cried others when we triumphed later on.

'Not at all,' we smirked, after pocketing prize conker (stick, marble, stone, tin can), and striding from the scene.

And then finding ourselves striding, a few years later, amid whirring fans, tightening ropes, and shouts in varied languages, including a variety of English never heard before. When travelling to a foreign land it is sensible to purchase a phrase-book, the better to understand its natives. Therefore, herewith a glossary of terms and initials likely to be encountered at a

Balloons do only travel with the wind, but some balloonists are (almost always) better at flying near the chimneys and dropping their markers down them.

competition meet (and to be heard in between the more ordinary forms of talk, that is if there is any ordinary talk at all).

PERSONNEL

Competition Director
The task-setter, briefing-giver, score-overseer, and principal receiver of complaints.

Observer
No mere bystander, but the official recorder appointed to see fair play, report infringements, detect inconsiderate behaviour.

Jury-person
There must be three if protests are to be investigated. They must be officially approved for major events, or selected randomly from amongst all pilots for minor ones.

Safety Officer
Directly responsible to official authority for major competitions, and always important even in the most minor.

TASKS

Judge-declared goal (JDG)
The director defines a target downwind of the launch site. Competitors must drop markers as near as possible to it.

Pilot-declared goal (PDG)
Same as JDG except that pilots choose their targets before taking off, these targets unknown to all other pilots. They must be more than a minimum distance from the launch site.

Hesitation waltz
Same as JDG (or even PDG), save that there are two targets, and the pilot can choose either during flight.

Fly-in
A reverse of JDG and PDG, with the launch site as the goal. Pilots therefore start a (minimum) distance from the launch field, and drop their markers near an X at the site.

Fly-on
Pilot chooses a second goal during flight, stating its position on the marker dropped at the first target.

Elbow
Pilot drops two markers, aiming for a maximum change of course between the first and second.

Hare and hounds
The hare, a non-competitor, takes off a certain time before the others, the hounds then having to drop their markers near the hare's landing site.

Watership Down (Fly-in + Hare and Hounds)
The hounds take off from sites distant to the normal launch field, hoping to arrive there precisely when the hare is setting

off, thus bettering their chances of dropping markers at the hare's eventual landing spot.

Gordon Bennett Memorial

The target is outside a scoring area. Markers must be dropped as near as possible to the target but only within the scoring area.

Maximum distance

Fly as far as possible within a scoring area.

Minimum distance

Fly as short a distance as possible, with markers only to be dropped after a certain time has elapsed.

Calculated rate approach

Markers must be dropped within a scoring area but only during a previously defined span of time.

Director's whim

The director can increase/decrease his/her personal popularity by creating any variant of the traditional tasks which happen to enter his or her fiendish mind.

There is now no longer excuse for getting your PDG mixed up with your elbow, or a hare and hounds with a fly-in and fly-on. Even competitors have been known to forget in which competition they are competing, thereby dropping their markers near an X but outside the scoring area, or concentrating so hard on dropping the marker that they drop their balloon into some swamp/thicket/apiary/forest which happens to be nearby. It is not the winning, so they say, but the taking part. It is also not the taking apart (of something) for thinking only of the winning.

Despite the keen and determined sense of competition one extra and important aim, according to an official promoter of this cause, is 'to reinforce friendship among aeronauts of all nations'. Coincidentally it may do nothing of the sort. During a Dutch event I was encouraged by a son to 'go for it', in short to win. Normally I find it pleasanter to see the X, to disregard it and fly onwards, particularly if the experience is being supreme (which it often is), the passengers are fun (which they often are) and there is lots of daylight left (which may well be the case). What is the point of curtailing the experience by trying to land near a couple of cloth strips positioned 2,000 feet below? Better by far to carry on, to savour the enjoyment, and then to applaud wholeheartedly at prize-giving time.

Hare and hounds, Bristol. The hare balloon is in front, and the oddest bunch of hounds ever to be seen are attempting to land nearest to the hare's landing spot.

But the 'go for it' persisted, as youngsters have been known to do. So I went for it, for a particular road, and for a landing as near as possible to that portion of macadam winding through the Dutch countryside. Alas, but it was a form of bog in which I arrived, this thinly disguised with reeds and heavy with the smell of permanent decay. No sane aeronaut would ever have chosen such a touch-down spot, it so blatantly unsuitable (and damp and difficult for retrieve), but it lay next to the selected roadway marked on all our maps. After my touch-down the mosquitoes whined, some moorhens scuttled, and amazing gases bubbled from the sogginess beneath, but I had come to earth (of sorts) only 50 metres (or fathoms) from the all-important roadway which I could plainly see. Prize-giving therefore loomed before my eyes, even if no means loomed for leaving the slough into which I had arrived.

Help arrived in the very considerable person of an extremely strong Dutch policewoman. She waded through the swamp without a moment's pause. She arrived, hardly breathless, at our basket-side (while we on board just stood there, as balloonists have to do, the combined weight necessary to counter buoyancy). Our tremendous saviour clamped her fists around convenient ropes, and was soon pulling us along the track – this still bubbling excitedly – which she had bludgeoned through the reeds to reach our landing place. In no time at all – from our perspective – the basket containing all of us was placed upon the road. For good measure, having learned it was our goal, she then thumped us down upon its central, once-white line. There she smiled from ear to ear, and so did we, most gratefully.

As we deflated the balloon, a solid road so preferable to quagmire of any kind, she signed a 'witness document' which demanded 'impartial evidence' of our landing site. In a bold and flowing script (as bold and flowing as she had been in that awesome swamp) she declared not only that we had landed on the road but on its central line. My son, who arrived as this lady was departing, gave me a congratulatory pat (which I treasure to this day).

'Well done,' he said; 'You're bound to win this time.'

Not so. Forget the reinforcement of friendship. Forget the amity alleged to exist between aeronauts of all nations. There were, as we discovered when being de-briefed, *five* other pilots who had landed on that central line, who had testimonials from all manner of worthy citizens, and who looked at me

unblinkingly when I chided them for possible subterfuge.

'We had, how you say, good chance,' said one.

'Vot luck,' said another.

Vot ein bunch of crooks, I muttered to myself, before remembering – with a modest twinge – my own slight indiscretion. Came the prize-giving, and my son – as youngest guest – was chosen to select the winner's ticket from six paper slips within a hat.

'Go for it,' I whispered, as he left his seat.

And that is what he did. Never before had I won anything, and he and I were the proudest pair that evening. We had gone for it, and we had won. He never learned about the swamp, and I never understood how he had pulled my number from the hat, but what is a little deceit among father and son, among international aeronauts, among individuals busily reinforcing friendship as they compete to win the prize?

Back now to the real competitions, to real competitors, and to real observance of the rules. Those Dutch occasions were fun, but they were not what the Germans call *echt* and we call proper. We foreigners always knew the Dutch would win, nine times out of ten, whatever the rules. I once landed, carelessly, just before the deadline when all balloonists had been instructed to be back upon the ground, and realised my error the moment I hit the cow-pat freshly made for me. From it I saw a balloon high up, some 2,000 feet high up, which could not possibly land before the appointed time. Of course it would be the winner, and of course it was.

'Perhaps you did not understand the briefing,' said its pilot afterwards.

I might indeed have dropped off, after the hour on meteorology, the hour on paperwork procedure, and the hour on *règlements*, but I loved those Dutch occasions and had no wish to change one iota of their ways. For me, and my sort of competitor, they were perfection, relegating combat and contest to the film kind where all is make-believe. No one worried greatly, if at all, either before, during or after those flights over what are called the Netherlands. We guests loved the sense of occasion, the amazing music, the speeches, the meals, and – oh yes – the competitions as we strove, in theory, to gain some goal.

I realised the strength of Dutch indoctrination when, at the second major meet in Albuquerque, they appointed me a juryman. I was able to wander proudly, hidden behind a badge

Flying for a target is difficult. Dropping the marker is difficult. The whole business is difficult, but irresistible – for some.

of office, and wonder what kind of adjudication might come my way. It eventually arrived in the form of a snowstorm. Several balloons were up at the time, busily competing, when out of a sky of shimmering blue there came another of shimmering white. I imagined (rightly, as it happened) that the airborne pilots could see as little as I could see when seated snugly inside my jury-car. Turning on the windscreen-wipers I wondered what might be happening up there in all that white. Some of the airborne pilots, as I later learned, opted for descent. Others, knowing air contained fewer perils than pieces of unseen ground, preferred to stay aloft. Those pieces of unseen ground would surely stay unseen until only a second or two, at most, before they were encountered.

In time, a matter of 15 minutes or so, the storm passed. The Albuquerque sky abruptly shimmered blue once more, permitting the airborne lot to see and then to reach their goal. The descenders had arrived in no end of unfriendly destinations – all memorable but none lethal – and this lack of injury permitted these unhappy individuals to hurry my way and seek out the jury-car.

'Visibility has to be 5 nautical miles,' said one.

'It has to be 1,000 feet above and 1,000 feet below the balloon,' said another.

'Those who carried on flying should be penalised,' said a third.

'It wasn't fair,' said a fourth, summing up their sense of grievance (with an utterance evoking days long since gone, along with shorts and blazers).

Holland then came to my aid. A sense of disregard for *règlements* swam before my eyes. Memories of flagrant breach of stern instruction arrived pell-mell. How brave of the snow-men to have carried on, to have been rewarded with clarity after complete obscurity. How risky were all those landings when each choice of landing site had been handed to the gods. And how pernickety of that protesting mob to talk with such vehemence of VFR and nautical miles, of visual flight and written rules.

'So what?' was the gist of my reply.

With a thump of dismay upon the jury-car they moved away, muttering to each other about a 'valid protest' being taken to higher authority. At prize-giving I applauded the winning snow-men and earned, alas, further rebuke from the gentry who had landed – in my opinion – both recklessly and quite unnecessarily. Perhaps jury-men should never applaud – at least out loud. Perhaps also they should never have enjoyed the more casual style of conflict which I had learned, between the windmills,

above the dykes, and on the polders of the Netherlands. Nevertheless (after handing back the jury-car, and becoming a civilian once again) I did accept that, if there are to be rules, they might as well be obeyed, if possible, than discarded totally.

M odern competitive hot air ballooning does adhere to rules. The observers exist to ensure that it does. Juries spend long hours discussing protests, before concluding – Solomon-like – with wise adjudication. For major international events the CIA (chief governing body of all sport ballooning) provides not only a jury selection procedure but a list of approved jurors. A safety officer, also directly responsible to the CIA, is appointed.

As for the tasks there are several, or even many, in any major competition. More than one may be flown on each flight, and each is scored independently. The more tasks which can be achieved, either overall or on single flights, 'the more challenging (everything) becomes and helps to ensure a better competition', according to some official wording. The aim 'is to

even out the elements of luck', to make certain that 'consistent performance' is properly rewarded. It is up to the director to choose which tasks will be most suitable for the weather that either is occurring or is expected to occur.

As for the competitors they must first attend a briefing and, according to the same formal instruction, 'receive all the relevant met and task data, including time and distance limits, etc'. It is arguable that pilots win events not so much by flying them as by planning what best to do even before becoming airborne. In multi-task flights this is particularly important. Starting off wrongly almost guarantees carrying on wrongly, while starting off correctly – although guaranteeing nothing – does at least increase the chances of doing well later on.

There is also the dilemma concerning take-off time. Competition directors arrange (usually) that all balloons ascend within a limited period, thus equalising opportunity; but, from each competitor's viewpoint, is it best to start at the beginning or at the end of this allotted span? To be early means taking off before the weather alters significantly. To be late means gaining the advantage of seeing where earlier balloons are travelling, and at what speed at what height. Sometimes, of course (with humans and lemmings not entirely different species), everyone waits, causing an erratic scramble before the allotted time expires.

The markers which must be dropped (in JDGs, fly-ins and fly-ons, for example) can also pose problems of their own. In general they are brightly-coloured streamers attached to sandbags each weighing 70 grams (not too severe for landing upon ground-based heads). It is difficult, as military bomb-aimers have always known, dropping them accurately if they have to fall from any altitude. They are heavy (relative to thistledown) but are still blown by the wind for all the time before they hit the ground.

Those who choose to spit from their airborne basket (these choosers more numerous than might be presupposed) learn this basic truth, causing them – alas – to spit and spit again, the better to enhance their aim. The final throwing, dropping, and aiming of markers is no less troublesome than is the steering of balloons towards the point where throwing, dropping, and aiming become so critical. Occasionally forgotten, but always vital, is the fact that markers must be dropped where they can be located. There is no point in brilliantly, cunningly and

The aiming point is easy enough to see, whether Cross or Chimney, but only the very skilled (and lucky and persistent) come close.

triumphantly depositing that weighted nylon if no observer is ever going to find it among the brambles/forest/garbage dump in which it then arrived. 'A lost marker can earn no score' states the official proclamation.

The rules, with all their talk of manoeuvring, aiming, following and even overtaking, can make the sport of aeronautic competition sound as if balloons have suddenly acquired steering wheels, accelerators, brakes and the means, which yachts possess, of travelling somewhere other than downwind. This is not true, of course; but, unlike sailing boats, they can be placed at the precise altitude where wind will serve them best.

It *is* true that winds in the northern hemisphere travel more to the right at height (and more to the left in the southern hemisphere). It is *also* true that higher winds move faster in either hemisphere. As with all rules it is the exceptions which make them more intriguing. Thermals play local havoc with wind direction, with their hot air rising and gyrating. Inversions occur when temperature reduction with height becomes temperature *increase* with height, disturbing air flow as a

have effect quite a long way from the sea.

The sun's warmth, the change from night to day, and the Earth's rotation are all at the root of atmospheric behaviour over the surface of the land. The type of land, whether flat, hilly, jagged, dry, wet, forested, open or any other variation, influences all the general rules. So too do man-made things, that town, those walls, those concrete deserts spread out down below. It is up to the aeronaut, the competitive aeronaut, to sort out what is happening, and why it happened, and what might happen next, if the marker is to be dropped within sight, or near, or even on the cross marked out upon the ground.

These atmospheric antics can be fun to savour even without the impetus of a competition. Perhaps it is suddenly realised that a friend's house lies a couple of hours downwind – if the wind is being reasonable and likely to be consistent on that particular day. The aim is therefore to fly directly above that friend's house. In order to achieve what might seem impossible – with such an unsteerable thing as a balloon – there is a procedure which can (sometimes) work. First draw a line on the map from starting point to destination. If already airborne the

consequence. Katabatic winds, travelling faster down hill-slopes, can be sudden, prolonged or seemingly non-existent. Their counterparts, the anabatic winds, can also forget what they are supposed to do, and either do or do not travel faster up the slopes. Sea-breezes are generally more reliable, travelling landwards with greater intensity as the day progresses, and as the land heats up, but their direction veers with time and may almost be parallel to a coastline by late afternoon. They also

starting point must be correctly identified. Observe wind direction at ground level by looking for chimney stacks, bonfires, tell-tale ripples across the corn. Observe upper wind direction by noticing cumulus shadows travelling down below, and then assess their track. Notice one's own shadow, the distinctive balloon outline, travelling – probably – not in the same direction as either the cumulus (above) or the bonfire smoke (below) but – probably – somewhere in between.

It is also necessary to know, at every stage of the flight, whether the balloon's course over the ground is to the left or right of the track marked on the map. If to the left it is necessary to go nearer the cumulus (if the Coriolis force is being properly obeyed). If to the right go nearer the ground, and all that bonfire smoke. Finally, if everything has gone supremely well, cheer tremendously loudly when the friend's house looms in view, and louder still when passing directly overhead.

The friend will churlishly assume it was blind chance that his garden siesta could have been destroyed quite so raucously. He may never believe otherwise (at least out loud), but the friendly assortment up above, having concentrated so determinedly for two terrific hours, will know it was nothing of the sort. Besides, only winners can make the kind of cheer which shakes a dozing friend so very forcibly. And causes him, if all goes perfectly, to topple from his chair.

No such casual visitations are permitted during competitions, but their atmosphere is not as stern as might be supposed. Lindsay Muir, British balloonist, is a keen participant, and her reports tend to be light-hearted despite the airborne rivalry. She

task was set – JDG, JDG, fly-on… They seemed simple enough, but wind wasn't as indicated… No one got closer than 1,200 metres on either of the JDGs… some pilots ending even further away on their fly-ons. Miracle of miracles, Monday evening was also flyable… so, even if no more, we had enough tasks to declare the championship valid (2 flights, 4 tasks)'.

Tuesday proved impossible, but Wednesday was 'just about' flyable. The wind 'did its usual trick of misleading us which way it was blowing… The first JDG was set 5 metres from a canal bridge… the water wasn't really that cold… No one hesitated over the hesitation waltz… the wind was now increasing (causing) a few 'incidents' on landing… protests increased as flyable conditions decreased… trees still at an angle of 45 degrees, but decreased for an evening flight… a double hesitation waltz was set… wind suddenly shifted, and we ended up with over 90 degrees of steerage, making all of the goals achievable… Saturday was the best slot all week… A JDG was to be followed by a PDG… but only markers dropped within 30 metres of a yellow road would score… All in all 11 tasks were completed in five flights, despite the gloomy predictions of

was at the 1992 Nationals, for example, this event held to discover the best (and worst) of British at that time. There were 24 entrants, a number which promptly became 23 after the initial briefing, the weather looking none too good. Other prospects seemed better, such as 13 'real ales' at the nearby hotel.

With the start of the competition the beer was left behind, along with normal prose. 'The day dawned flyable and a triple

hurricane whatshername having undue influence.'

Moreover there were always those 13 real ales, particularly on

There is a grace in flying through the air. There is often mayhem after each meeting with the ground, intentionally or otherwise, and the disturbance merrily continues even after becoming airborne once again.

Tuesday, Thursday, Friday and, of course, Saturday following the prize-giving. For the record (on what was a memorable week, for flyers as well as publican) the first three were: Bareford D. 8,787 points, Gabriel N. 8,734, and Bridge I. 8,647. At the other end were: Percival J. 3,713, Mueller M. 3,711, and McCoy T. 2,240. The report's author, Muir L., scored a creditable 5,343, tactfully midway between top and bottom.

The Americans have been holding national championships since 1963, a mere three years since Ed Yost had coaxed ONR-1 into the air. The British, more belatedly (as there were no hot air balloons in those early 1960s), did not start their 'nationals' until 1975. A couple of years earlier the Americans had organised the 'World's First Hot-Air Balloon Championship'. This was held at Albuquerque, New Mexico, and Britain followed suit in 1977 when it played host – at Castle Howard, Yorkshire – to the third such championship. The Swedes did likewise – at Uppsala – in 1979, and – for the fourth time in a row – Americans won the event. By then the major forms of competition had been firmly established, with individual nations holding their own 'nationals' when they saw fit, and the 'worlds' taking place every other year.

There have been a few rival confrontations, the longing to compete not – presumably – sufficiently assuaged by nationals and worlds. Tom Heinsheimer, American pressure-balloon expert (and one-time Atlantic hopeful, together with Malcolm Forbes), decided in 1979 to resurrect the Gordon Bennett long-distance races after their lapse of 41 years. Europeans were invited, and various Europeans attended, but all were disconcerted to discover that some Americans had built some very large balloons, fashioned from novel materials, with every intention of winning the event. Take-off was from the vicinity of the old *Queen Mary*, solidly docked at Long Beach, California, and an American team did indeed win that year's prize.

The winners of all subsequent talk about the competition were, undoubtedly, the Poles. First notification of their attendance was a disturbed phone call from Los Angeles airport: 'Some gentlemen here are short of documentation, but have

It is possible, very possible, to concentrate so determinedly upon the target that the actual ground is quite forgotten, with all contact earning penalties.

made us understand they are balloonists ...'. More trouble ensued when this team became airborne. There are 20 airports of varying sizes within the L.A. area, causing all of the Gordon Bennett pilots to receive fairly strict instructions. Only after nightfall was it realised that the Polish balloon was still airborne, and its flight-path would take it over LAX, biggest airport of them all. Police authorities scrambled a searchlight-equipped helicopter, discovered a Polish-speaking policeman, and managed via the machine's loud-hailing system (normally for quelling desperadoes) to inform the Polish crew that the garbage dump over which they happened to be flying was not only suitable for a touch-down but imperative as a touch-down place. Everyone sighed heavily, not least at LAX, when the Poles obeyed the positive instruction assaulting them from the dark.

For a while the new-style Gordon Bennetts continued to operate from California, and Americans in large balloons always did well, but Europe increasingly resented the New World's interpretation of the ancient competition. For a while there were two Gordon Bennetts, one in the USA and one in Europe, but the Europeans eventually prevailed. The single long-distance race is now an annual event, and has been performed happily, save for the dreadful year (1995) when a Belarus helicopter gunship shot down a Virgin Islands balloon, killing both men on board.

Polish aeronauts achieved different renown during the Parisian celebrations of 1983 commemorating the flights of 1783. It had been arranged that the Place de la Concorde (adjacent to the Tuileries Gardens, take-off site for Professor Charles) would serve as prestigious launch-place for a dozen gas balloons from several nations. This event could have been a mere celebration, extolling 200 years of flight, but it became transformed into a long-distance competition. On the actual day it was very nearly transformed into nothing whatsoever, the sky turning black just when all balloons had received their fill of gas. There were thunder, lightning, gust and rain, with the rain most memorable, it drenching everything and everyone in liberal style.

When it ceased, abruptly as if a tap had been discharging, the eerie sky was half blue and half black, with the storm moving elsewhere. A pure white balloon, carrying two Americans, Maxie Anderson and Don Ida, then ascended, looking quite as miraculous – with white against black – as Jacques Charles's colourful aerostat had done all those years ago. In more leisurely fashion, and less impulsively, the other balloons then ascended, their pilots entirely drenched, but their enthusiasm undimmed, as they left to join the air – save, we suddenly realised, for a solitary balloon which still stood upon the take-off site, most buoyantly but quite bereft of clientele.

The two Polish pilots, it transpired, had returned to their hotel. After taking a bath there and putting on a dry set of clothes they returned within an hour or two to attend to their balloon. In a most happy fashion, not influenced one jot by policemen urging them to go and giving them instruction (determinedly in French), they ascended. They then flew in quite a different airstream to the others, and of course they won.

When news was arriving of their victory, and judges were affirming they had committed no sin by changing clothes or bathing, news also arrived that Maxie Anderson and Don Ida had both died in Germany. Their quick-release system, between envelope and basket, had allegedly proved faulty, permitting their basket to be separated when too high above the ground. Only five years earlier Maxie had been revelling in the Atlantic conquest when he, Ben Abruzzo and Larry Newman had ballooned from America to France. Before long Ben Abruzzo was also to die in a more ordinary aircraft accident. Larry Newman did not die in his five attempts to balloon around the world, all five ending speedily and all five looking (to many an outsider) as if the pilot might succumb as well. Fate had been very kind to *Double Eagle II*, making that trans-Atlantic venture seem so effortless. Fate then had a change of heart, or so it seemed to those who think this way.

Putting talk of death firmly to one side, and returning to happy competition, the 1996 Saga International Balloon Fiesta can serve as antidote. The Japanese, not averse to competition, have been holding events at Saga since 1981. In 1996, their enthusiasm gaining momentum, they decided within that year's jamboree to promote the Pacific Cup, the Ladies World Cup, the Pacific Championship, the Japanese National Championship, the final of the Honda Grand Prix, and the first stage of the Australia-Japan Challenge Cup. It would be a sad spectator who did not, somehow, become involved in such intensive rivalry.

Once again Lindsay Muir, determined competitor, can be our guide, hopefully now entirely comprehensibly. The event 'started in earnest with a hesitation waltz and a fly-on... Conditions were typically Saga, slow and variable... I managed a 46 cm drop... The following morning winds were strong but, as there was a good inversion, we still managed to fly a triple – PDG, fly-in, fly-on... It was a question of take off, hurl the markers towards the goals as you whizz past them, and land before you run out of land... The wind had eased on the following morning, permitting another triple – fly-in, JDG, fly-on... the best result achieving only 55m, with most pilots scoring 300-400m...'.

And so on, with windy days, Saga days, PZs, ten pilots scoring 'less than 1.5 m' on one task, and Uwe Schneider, of Germany, pronounced at week's end as the winner. He, having done a 2 m and then a 16 m drop, then 'proceeded to fly back to the launch site and landed on the launch point – thus showing what it takes to be a champion'. Who said that balloons can only travel with the wind? Plainly Mr Schneider can make wind travel with the balloons, or solely with his balloon? The final national order of the top ten was: Germany, Hungary, Japan, USA, USA, Germany, Japan, USA, Japan, and Australia. Britain's best performance was by Crispin Williams – 15th, while L Muir, ecstatic and undaunted as ever, was 25th (out of 105 competitors). Putting icing on her cake was her achievement of first place in the Ladies World Cup, helping her to consider it had been the best Saga 'for years'.

For all those who like creating simplicity, such as rafts, these being the cheapest and most straightforward kind of boat, it is necessary to issue a caution. Some day someone will shout: 'Go for it, and may the best raft win'. A warning is important because, however much the raft-builder may have thought that a raft's charm depended entirely upon an inability to go faster than the water on which it sits, its constructor may heed the cry and start to feel competitive.

'My raft is better and faster than your raft', says someone else, and then the race is on.

So watch out! The spirit of rivalry can take hold! Raft-builders of the world will meet, and will annually compete. They will compete yet more avidly, and respectfully, if they chance to see a rafteer named Schneider rafting disconcertingly, but convincingly (and winningly), quite the other way.

CHAPTER 9

The showmen

'It is plainly wrong to think of balloons solely as vehicles from which to look at the passing countryside... The desire to jump from baskets, to parachute from them, to hang from them at the end of a rubber band, is very strong – in some.'

PERHAPS SOMEONE CALLED IT A STUNT, a piece of showmanship, a *bon coup*, when the first two aeronauts ascended over Paris in 1783. Yet more certainly many others talked of showmanship when later balloonists ascended on horseback, launched fireworks, or descended by parachute. The very act of aviation in those early days was a piece of theatre. Those pioneers were artistes, often charging an entrance fee, and being harangued by the attendant crowd whenever a performance failed to satisfy.

So what price these days, when ballooning is still – in part – a piece of showmanship and still – at times – accompanied by stunts? The average balloonist (if there is such a one) is happy enough for people to watch the spectacle of ascent, of flight and of descent, but is likely to be resentful if the term stunt is

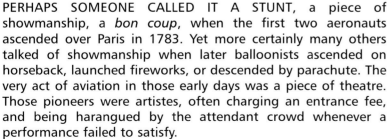

Even when balloon flying was in its infancy the aeronauts ascended on horseback, let off fireworks, or fell with parachutes. So what else is new?

used for such an ordinary occupation. A stunt is something out of the ordinary, a spectacular display, a showy performance, a hazardous enterprise. Land dwellers, with both feet rooted firmly to the earth, might assert that ballooning itself is extraordinary, spectacular, showy, and hazardous, but the one whose feet happen to be airborne is liable to disagree. The flight is merely a flight, of an ordinary and unamazing kind.

The division between conventional ballooning and something meriting the name of stunt seems to lie in the basic intent. Is an activity for benefit of its participants or for an audience? A stunt

quietly performed, out of sight and unrecorded, is not worthy of that title. A pleasure cruise, giving joy to all on board which happens to provide a spectacle, is also unworthy. On the other hand a stunt (whose etymological origins lie in US college talk) may be fun, and probably is fun, but it is ostentatious, a piece of advertisement, and a risky undertaking with the risk well publicised. At an elementary level it is standing on the basket rim, the better to wave at a crowd below. At a higher level (in every sense) it is parachuting from the basket or dropping with a hang-glider. At an extreme level, involving abseiling, tight-rope walking, free-falling, bungee-jumping or all four of them, it is emphatically Ian Ashpole.

Without doubt he is performing for the camera. As like as not there is one in a nearby helicopter, a few in and around the

Not everyone has a file labelled 'Daft Ideas Hatched Late At Night' but those who do so tend to take them seriously even in the morning.

basket, and probably one on his head as well. Therefore film and photographs both showed him tight-rope walking (for heaven's sake) between two balloons which were flying a couple of miles above the ground. This first 'aircraft to aircraft tight-rope walk' occurred well out of sight of ground-based humans but, as Ian disarmingly phrased it, 'there's no point in carrying out a stunt like this if you don't capture it on film'. The walk was also out of sight for Ian as, for good measure, he performed it with a blindfold on his eyes. Of course.

The 'tight-rope' was a bar attached to each balloon at basket-

level, and the balloons (piloted by Richard Turnbull and Chris Dunkley) were united by a length of light-weight aluminium. A 15 ft balancing bar, standard equipment for tight-rope walkers even at ground level, was loosely attached (by a thin line) to each balloon, partly because it is unsatisfactory dropping 15 ft balancing bars on the English countryside. At 10,500 feet above Herefordshire Ian began his walk, and successfully reached the other basket. The pilots had to trim their craft, and not fly too high or low, as the weight of one human (for that is what Ian is) was shifted from one basket to another. Having crossed satisfactorily it was then occasion, naturally, for Ian to travel back whence he had come. During this second walk he tripped, stumbled, seemed to regain his balance, tripped again and – inevitably – fell, with cameras everywhere recording this dilemma, a dilemma as well rehearsed as all the rest.

Parachutes these days are so slim-line they are practically invisible – which makes the sight of someone falling better still. Those of us who walk on top of 2 ft walls know that, even if we slip, we will survive to tell the tale. Ian (presumably) feels similarly secure, with a parachute (or two) always somewhere about his person. He never, as it were, leaves home without one. Most of his exploits, swinging from trapezes, swinging from anything which comes to hand, tend to end up with him swinging from a parachute. And then landing gently at some convenient location, having steered his way back to earth from wherever it was, and whatever he was doing, a long way up above.

Such as abseiling higher and for longer than anyone else had ever done. He reckons he has a Daft Ideas Hatched Late at Night file, and this was one of them. He acquired a rope, 10 mm thick and 650 ft long, which seemed suitable for descent. This was attached to a balloon which then ascended to 12,000 feet over Chateau d'Oex in Switzerland, the sort of height where reduced oxygen levels can make 'ideas hatched late at night' seem more reasonable. For some reason the rope could not be deployed in its entirety, but had to be 'self-deployed' from a large rucksack attached to Ian's left leg. Another minor upset occurred when the descending device (through which an abseiler's rope passes to control descent) became so hot that it started to burn the rope. No problem. There is always the trusty, slim-line, ever-obliging parachute, a sure-fire system for leaving any difficulty which might arise somewhere up above.

What is so wrong with a basket that a few of us long to leave it and reach the ground some other way?

'At an extreme level, involving abseiling, tight-rope walking, free falling, bungee-jumping or all four of them, it is Ian Ashpole.'

Abseiling for 650ft broke all records, such as those achieved by mere mountaineers; so what about bungee jumping? Someone, somewhere, and sometime in the past (no doubt late at night) had earlier considered rubber sufficiently sound to make jumping off bridges, or from cranes, more fun than it had been in earlier days. Tie one end of a piece of elastic to your ankles, attach the other to a bridge, measure the distance from bridge to ground *very carefully*, make allowance for the rubber's stretch, and then jump, achieving all the thrill of a suicidal leap without the upsetting penalty of death. How much better, therefore, to forget about bridges, cranes and the like, and think about balloons. Once again Ian Ashpole was more than two miles above Herefordshire, and once more he leaped into the record books. His bungee jump was undertaken from 12,610ft.

The highest bungee jump. First reach 12,000 feet. Then attach elastic to your ankles. Then jump, with a friend to record the action.

It is plainly staid to think of balloons solely as enchanting vehicles from which to look, in the company of friends, at the passing countryside. It is equally wrong to think of baskets solely as suitable containers from which to make those observations, with occupants having no more wish to leave them prematurely than depart from cars still speeding along a road. The desire to jump from baskets, to parachute from them, to hang from them at the end of a rubber band, is plainly very strong – in some. Rory McCarthy, wealthy hang-glider enthusiast (if that is not a contradiction), has taken off a hundred times beneath balloons, but has only landed with them once. For the other 99 he preferred to jump (and then descend some other way).

There is also a wish which exists (with some) to jump from them and then come back again. If this sounds impractical, or plain impossible, the mystery can be savoured a little longer while Mike Howard, its organiser, tells the tale.

'After 20 minutes of climbing we had finally reached 13,500 feet. The climb rate was down to 50 feet per minute, so we took the decision to initiate the descent.

At 12,000 feet the first two parachutists left the basket. Thanks to some clever packing they were under canopy within 100 feet. This meant they could start to make their approaches almost immediately. At 11,000 feet the third parachutist was out.

We had calculated that each parachutist had two minutes to get back in. As the balloon was passing 9,000 feet we still had not got anyone back in, and it looked like we were never going to do it. Then, out of nowhere, Steve Blee made a perfect approach which finished with a perfect landing on the safety net just below the bottom of the basket. I then lowered the safety line which Steve connected to himself before climbing into the basket.

Steve Rickets (also of the Red Devils) was next to make an attempt. His approach looked good but a little low, and he only just caught the bottom of the net.

Unfortunately the two of us who had stayed in the basket were unable to reach his chute. In all the scenarios previously discussed we had decided this was probably the most dangerous situation. We therefore lowered a safety line and this worked perfectly. Halfway up the net Steve (Rickets) managed to bundle up his chute and climb with it.'

That had all taken time, but the third parachutist positioned himself for an approach. Unfortunately the landing net had become twisted, causing this third man to be motioned away. By then, with altitude down to 3,500 feet and with time running out, it was decided that two re-arrivals had been sufficient, the previous record having been one such return. Mike Howard and the two Steves had therefore successfully doubled that figure (and, no less successfully, showed the story of their achievement on BBC TV).

Perhaps another and current definition of a stunt is whether the exploit is seen on television. Many a major endeavour these days is not considered to have happened unless it enters a million sitting-rooms via the auspices of some transmitter. Way back in 1963, when I and Douglas Botting had flown a gas balloon across the European Alps, we were financed and recorded by a team from the BBC. To float serenely over the Eiger, so desperate (and often lethal) a challenge for advanced mountaineers, was bizarre. Up there we munched bananas, chewed chicken, ate grapes, sipped drink and occasionally gazed at the famous northern face while down there, although invisible from our vantage point, were two dead Spanish climbers for whom the ascent had, one week earlier, proved too great an obstacle.

It takes three days to reach the top of Africa's Mount Kilimanjaro, its visitors puffing wearily through the lower forests, and then up at dawn on Day 3 to climb the final scree before each day's warmth melts the ice which binds the fractured rock conveniently in place. For Alan and Joan Root, first to float over this volcanic peak by hot-air balloon, it took them but an hour to reach 20,000 feet, and then to float across a summit where earthlings well below them were panting over ice and snow. The sight of Kilimanjaro, wrote Alan in his TV commentary, makes 'any balloonist worth his basket' wish to fly across it. Not everyone may wish (or their wishes may be trampled by 3 am anxieties over what might come to pass) but television and other forms of sponsorship do help at least to pay for exploits more costly than normal kinds of flight.

Almost inevitably, if thoughts of flying over mountains are in the air, someone will dream of Everest, highest of them all. Equally inevitably such an enterprise, apart from its other difficulties, is going to be expensive. There were one or two endeavours, failing at Kathmandu or earlier, but in 1990 a Japanese balloon carrying three men was heading purposefully towards the highest peak on Earth. Suddenly it was becalmed, and an early landing had to be achieved. It was neither a good one nor in a good place. One man's femur was broken, and he was fortunately dragged clear before, with propane leaking, everything caught fire. After a difficult time at 18,500 feet, wrapped in their parachutes to combat the cold, all three men were rescued, with Round 1 definitely having been won by the mountain.

Round 2 became protracted, with every form of setback, much changing of personnel, much changing of everything (such as the deployment of two balloons rather than one), until a considerable assortment of people, two balloons and lots of cameras were at Gokyo, 18,000 feet above sea level. The year was 1991, or 67 years after George Mallory and Andrew Irvine had famously disappeared near Everest's peak, 58 years since British biplanes had flown over the mountain, 38 years since Edmund Hillary and Norgay Tenzing had been first to stand upon it, 16 years since Doug Scott and Dougal Haston had been first Britons to do so, 13 years since anyone had climbed it without oxygen, and one year since the Japanese team had been lucky to escape from their balloon alive.

The plan at Gokyo was that both balloons should take off in reasonable proximity so that each could photograph the other. 'We had agreed upon a 20-second interval,' wrote Leo Dickinson later, but it did not work out like that. He and Chris Dewhirst were to be in one balloon, with Andy Elson and Eric Jones in the other. Due to misunderstanding (which some believe may have been deliberate) the departure interval was nearer two minutes than the 20 seconds which had been planned. This meant, when the balloons separately encountered 60 mile-an-hour winds at altitude, that each quickly became a speck in the other's viewfinders.

Instead of a dual enterprise it was a brace of singletons, but both did brilliantly. At 34,000 feet, and speeding along at a mile a minute, they crossed the forbidding summit with one of the greatest views this planet has to offer on every side. To achieve better pictures Leo stood *outside* the basket on 200 rupees worth of plywood, and did so for much of the journey. When Everest was some 80 miles behind them, and they were above a flattish portion of Tibet, it was occasion for the landing. Perhaps as punishment for having jumped the gun, for being first to cross the peak, Leo and Chris had a damaging time. With fate working overtime to even up the score, and as reward for being beaten to the post, Andy and Eric had a gentle upright touchdown 10 miles further on.

Yes, it was a stunt. Yes, it was filmed and then transmitted. And, yes, it was exceptionally expensive, the figure of $2.5 million being near the mark. It was a piece of showmanship, a *bon coup*, a spectacular display, a hazardous enterprise, but no less demanding of courage, of skill and expertise, than every other such adventure since the first two men in Paris had astonished the world by ascending above the roof-tops for all to see. For those whose feet are planted more firmly on good and solid ground there is one question which still stays dominant – 'Just what will happen next?'.

CHAPTER 10

The people carriers

Many say that it is the dream of a lifetime to go up in a balloon, and many a balloonist makes a good living fulfilling all such dreams. More people are currently becoming airborne in this fashion than ever before in ballooning's lengthy history.

SHE HAD NOT BEEN CONSPICUOUS BEFOREHAND. There were 10 passengers to go on board, and the business of manoeuvring limbs, bodies, hats and bags over the basket's edge had prevented detailed examination of which items belonged to whom. There were shrieks, and laughs, apologies and grunts, before all 10 were standing within the wickerwork waiting for their flight. They were an amalgam of humanity, a gathering, an assortment of clientele who had each paid a sum for one journey by balloon. For the rest of us on board they had not yet become separate and distinct individuals.

Besides it was an exquisite evening. Britons spend much time and energy travelling to other lands – for more sunshine, less rain, greater warmth – and can forget there is nothing quite so perfect as a perfect British day. The air has a softness which nowhere else can emulate. The land has more shades of green than can seem reasonable, each vying to be the very best, and each triumphant differently. Everything is harmony, the fields and trees, the hills and streams, and then the heron flapping home most wearily after a day of doing nothing but standing by the water's edge watching for signs of fish. The county was Wiltshire. The acres round about belonged to a stately home, and the home itself stood most correctly in the midst of all its land. As for the actual balloon ascent, which soon transported the 10 clients above the ground, that too was quite correct. The basket and its basketful moved upwards with a perfect grace.

She then let us know that she was on board. She was smaller than most, and her voice grated rather more than most, particularly in the message that it conveyed.

'I've forgotten my Kleenex,' she said, before opening her mouth again, in case we had not heard.

'Yes, I've forgotten my Kleenex, and it's down there on the ground.'

Nine people were promptly sympathetic, murmuring gently in tune with her dismay. One offered a small pack of tissues, neatly contained within its plastic foil. There was then more murmuring from the other eight that such a swift, kind and appropriate solution had been so promptly found. From hand to hand the package went until donated to the unhappy individual, so distraught in her distress.

'No,' she said, with quick dismissal; 'It's *my* box of Kleenex that I want, and it's on a wall down there.'

The pilot, as competent as any, was no more capable of flying backwards to the take-off site than of summoning one forlorn

Big Ben, the Houses of Parliament and much of London seen from the basket of a balloon hovering above Vauxhall.

box towards its owner. He saw she was about to speak again, presumably with the same stirring words, and turned on both burners to drown the irksome sound. Unfortunately, as he knew and others realised, the decibels were welcome but not the gain in height which they induced. It is nicest to be nearer to the ground, where the smells can be savoured, the lie of the land better understood, the rabbits seen more easily, the flight most wonderful and astonishing. *Force majeure* he turned the burners off, but *force* even more *majeure* she let loose again.

'You see, it's my husband. If he had any sense he would find the Kleenex, and take it to the car. But he probably won't, and the box will just sit there until, I suppose, someone else will take it home. I do wish I hadn't forgotten my Kleenex.'

Various other wishes were stirring, almost visibly, within that basket space, or maybe but a single wish uniformly felt. All scents of earth are harder to detect, each rabbit less fun, and the landscape less entrancing when there is tissue talk so very clear, and near. The flight had been transformed from heaven to its awesome counterpart. We did not collectively, and unanimously, throw her overboard. Perhaps we should have done, the occasion so overwhelmed with extenuating circumstance. We merely stood there, silent with our single thought and battered by the solitary cause of our multiple dismay.

I had not previously realised a balloon flight could ever be such a wretched undertaking. Even less had I understood that misery could be enhanced a hundredfold if the day is perfect, the air perfect, and all sights at their optimum. I merely knew I could never be a people carrier, a commercial operator giving flights for money, a transporter of individuals selected only by the cheques which they have signed. I would take friends, and friends of friends, but not other kinds of human who could kill, ye gods, the very best of England without being killed themselves.

Perhaps travel couriers, hotel managers, head waiters, airline stewards, bus conductors, tour operators and every form of people organiser already know – only too well – that every assorted barrel contains one rotten apple. Or even three. The couriers must have developed thick skins, or formulated cunning answers, to prevent them paying undue attention to the trouble-makers, the least deserving, the most obstreperous. After all – or so I assume – the majority is not complaining, and the majority should have the greater say, exert the greater

influence, swamp all minor interference before it gains a hold.

I learned something of this general truth when flying in Africa a short time later with what they call a safari balloon. Long before, and in 1962, when I had flown a gas balloon over bits of that same continent, such as its forbidding thorn trees, its untrodden forests, and its uninhabited regions, in the hope of seeing herd after herd of big game alleged to exist in the same general area, I had more frequently observed the underneaths of cu-nim clouds, the surfaces of soda lakes, and miles of savanna as far as eyes could see, with animals often in short supply. Or the balloon was being troublesome. Or life itself was thought likely to be ended – very likely to be ended – before the day itself expired.

Just once there was a herd beneath us, huge and magnificent, but the flights had not been the leisurely progress of my earlier imaginings. I had wanted wildebeest, zebras, gazelles, rhinos, elephants, buffaloes, hyenas, lions to be peacefully beneath me while I leant on a basket's rim giving my retinas the time of their lives. It had never been my intention to suffer mile-high bounces, rasp through skin-ravaging vegetation, hit rocks sideways, or land in amazement that death had not prevailed. All those memories of spines, spikes, cliffs, thunder-clouds and jungles had etched themselves more deeply than the fleeting four-footed spectacles we were, briefly, permitted to enjoy.

Therefore what price a modern balloon safari, with a competent pilot, a flight system clearly understood, and animals increasingly complacent about huge balloons in their fields of view? At Keekorok in the Maasai Mara I met a captain of such balloons, requested space in his basket, and asked how he handled his 'punters' in general and the awkward ones in particular.

Passenger-carrying means bigger baskets, sometimes with space for a dozen or so clientele. Phil Dunnington (right) and Cameron offerings.

'No problem,' was all he said.

With that we took off. It was early in the day, and the flight quickly became the leisurely progress of my old imaginings. There were zebras down there, and wildebeest, with gazelles forever prancing between them. Our pilot was sorting out some floor matter before quietly saying 'Elephants on the right'. I looked and looked. We all looked and looked, and eventually someone saw the very distant flapping of an ear.

'Good heavens!' I muttered to the floored pilot; 'That was clever.'

'Always elephants out there,' he whispered back; 'Giraffes to the left, if you can spot them.'

'Do you see the giraffes, over there,' I said silently to the young – and handsome – girl standing next to me.'

'Oh look, Daddy, there are giraffes over to the left.'

I was learning fast. The girl was happy because she had shown them to her father. The father was happy because his happy daughter had shown them first to him. He had then whispered the information to his wife, she still pleased at having been first to see the elephants. And so the news spread, everyone content with all the revelation. When the pilot did surface, his labour by the floor completed, he had a basketful of very happy passengers. They even pointed out the giraffes and elephants for him and he, cunning fellow, was dumfounded by their long-range skill. Any minor perturbations there might have been, any suspicions of complaint, were therefore drowned at once in the general joy.

One hour later, with photographic film all consumed, and with pleasure radiating merrily from everyone on board, the pilot announced that our landing might be soon. We were then travelling six feet or so above the ground, engaged on what one cheerful passenger had dubbed an entòmological safari; so I presumed our landing's imminence. Not so. From zero altitude (as near as dammit) the pilot shot us up 3,000 feet. There he gave stern warning about cameras and field-glasses. 'These are to be safely stowed,' he said. 'Spectacles should certainly be removed', and removed they were at once. The very needy were therefore plunged into an out-of-focus world, but they knew – we all knew – that the landing phase had now begun. Giraffes, elephants, and even insects were forgotten. Landing time was nigh.

Our pilot then vented a considerable quantity of air. In consequence we started to descend at a considerable speed. The apprehension mounted, it too becoming – well – considerable. I do not know if we overtook falcons making their own more leisurely way towards some lower offering, but I do know I have rarely descended quite so fast. At 500 feet our two burners were turned to maximum, thus serving to act as brakes. Very noisily they belched heat into the envelope. Would this be sufficient to break our fall? Would it? Would...? If not, what would be broken?

The descent did slacken, but was still fast. The ground loomed, becoming clearer by the second. There was utter silence on board. The jokes had finished. All talk had gone. Everyone looked ground-wards, each holding handling ropes as had been ordered. How sensible that cameras had been packed away! How far-sighted about spectacles! How very near the ground looked (either in focus or out)! How very near! How...! And then we hit, and bounced, and toppled, and fell, and soon were in a heap. The landing had been achieved.

'So why?' I asked the pilot afterwards; 'Why like an eagle bereft of normal sense?'

'Oh, they like it that way,' he answered; 'The punters like it good and firm.'

Plainly they did. They were now more radiant even than previously. What a flight it had been! What sights! As for the touch-down, that had been supreme! After breakfast, eaten while sitting on propane cylinders above the coarse grasses of the Maasai Mara, we were all returned to the hotel, most happily and content, talking of terror firmer as if first to make this weary joke (second only in profundity to the one about hot air).

'Well done,' I said to the pilot afterwards.

'Run-of-the-mill, really,' he replied; 'Just give them what they expect. Make them feel they've been luckier than most. Leave them to see all the animals first. Frighten them a bit. Hit them down hard, and you don't get any complaints. Same time tomorrow?'

With that he signed their (costing extra) T-shirts, ticked lists of all the animals seen (plus some others which had stayed invisible), sold videos and different bits and pieces before sending them on their way. The whole procedure had been superb. It seemed so easy, like any skill effortlessly portrayed. Perhaps I too could learn the art? Perhaps ... ? On second

More people in the basket also means a bigger balloon, but such bigger payloads (or loads of payers) mean bigger profits for the ones in charge.

thoughts no one had asked for Kleenex, their very own Kleenex which they had left behind.

'Thank you for showing me the giraffes,' said the young girl, a touch more handsome even than before (and Daddy somewhere else).

I looked at her more intently now. Could she ever, when grown more gnarled and ancient in her ways, worry that her Kleenex, her very own box of Kleenex, had been left behind? That thought then kept me silent, and soon she skipped away.

Flying passengers by balloon has become big business. That girl and her parents would help to spread the word. So too, I felt certain, the rest of that basket-load. The experience had been great, well worth the dollars or shillings which it had cost. Besides (always a powerful argument) when would those same individuals be in Africa once more? Perhaps never, and the opportunity to fly by balloon over big game might never again arise. So why not pay the extra, climb into a basket, see giraffes, elephants and all the rest before flying home, albeit conventionally (and slightly poorer), but aware that a chance for further and amazing novelty had not been thrown away.

In Britain (and other ballooning nations) passenger-flying is also big business, grossing – in Britain alone – £7,500,000, or so, each year. This is almost as much as the Cameron balloon factory turns over annually, with its 130 employees creating more balloons than any other enterprise. People, it would seem, do like being transported in groups over the land which they normally see either from roads or on foot. At more than £100 a go (or half as much again) they welcome the opportunity – even if the flight is over cows, fields, oak trees and soft hillsides, speckled here and there with sheep, rather than lions, water-holes, yellow-barked acacias and hyrax-covered rocks.

Towards the end of the 1980s it was realised, by balloonists as well as officialdom, that the existing system had grown too large for the relaxed manner in which it was operating. There was no problem for friends to be given rides, or extended family, or friends of all that family, or just friends of friends of friends, but the actual purchase of a flight by a stranger brought different obligations. Was the pilot competent? Was he properly insured and physically fit? If there was an accident would the innocent passengers have redress? If so, on what grounds?

Airline pilots or air-taxi operators have written responsibilities and must obey them. Should balloon pilots be any different when they too are taking cash?

No particular accident prompted the change in mood (or of the regulations) but that earlier casual attitude did have to be addressed. The British Association of Balloon Operators, a new group of extremely interested parties, helped to coordinate supplementary strictures. In essence no one could become such an operator (and take money) unless he/she:

♦ Had already been pilot-in-charge of balloons for 150 hours.

♦ Had passed a medical exam (costing about £100 a year).

♦ Had been 'type-rated' for the size of balloon to be flown

♦ Would keep detailed records of passenger's names and weights, of fuel carried and fuel consumed etc. for every fare-paying flight.

Each year BABO totals the number of flights flown plus passengers carried from all the compilations returned by all the various operators. Recently these have been:

Year	Flights	Passengers
1990	6,854	34,572
1991	8,604	45,886
1992	8,292	48,682
1993	9,494	60,800
1994	9,512	66,290
1995	10,269	71,953
1996	8,961	66,545
1997	9,362	74,059

Not only have such totals climbed during the 1990s, indicating that ballooning is still gaining in its appeal, but the average number of passengers flown per flight is increasing, with these numbers rising – during those same eight years – from 5.04 to 5.33 to 5.87 to 6.40 to 6.97 to 7.01 to 7.42 to 7.91. It is more economical – and more profitable as with giant aircraft – to pack in more passengers, and to fly with bigger baskets beneath even bigger balloons.

Although 50 or so passengers have occasionally been flown at once, as with the double-decker basket of the Nashua balloon,

Captive balloons for passenger rides, without the virtues or uncertainties of free flight, have also been gaining enthusiasts, just as they did a century ago.

these individuals have not been paying for their crowded passage through the air. No more than 19 people can be carried at any one time by the balloon operators. Above that number there is legal stipulation for 'cabin crew' to accompany the pilot. Whatever airline passengers may think, as they watch the staff shoving trolleys of food and drink towards their clientele, the primary purpose of such stewardship is for the 'safety and well-being' of those who are consuming all that stuff. No balloon operator – yet – wishes to pay for extra personnel, and each will continue to pack in more passengers (below the limit) to improve the bank account.

There will, presumably, come a time (long since reached with airlines) when passengers resent sardine-like concentration within the wickerwork. Once in Morocco I rode with a host of others, this flight for entertainment only. In order to look down upon rows and rows of olive and orange and lemon trees, all delectable in their symmetry, I had to peer round and over the others on board, getting glimpses through armpits and over chests or breasts. The eventual landing was a happy one, with yet more person-to-person mingling, and the experience had been good – as well as free. I therefore wondered if I might have been aggrieved at such bodily compression (so well known on London's Underground) had I previously donated a major hunk of money to the man in charge.

'A great flight!' I said later, when encountering a girl who seemed to be part of the retrieval team; 'You should have been on board.'

'But I was,' she said.

There is much to be said for travelling in a car rather than a bus.

It is a truism that regulations, once they get a grip, tend not to let go, with medical requirements a case in point. No one hopes for a pilot to succumb in flight, preventing further control by that individual, and therefore physical examinations have been initiated. Personally, I would rather a balloon commander dropped dead, and failed accordingly, than either a fixed-wing or helicopter pilot. Balloons left alone can make satisfactory landings, perhaps even bettering some managed by their owners, but other forms of crashing aircraft are more determined in their destruction should their captains slump forwards when in the driving seat.

To some extent the modern ballooning movement has clung to the coat-tails of the gliding authorities when assessing what should be done. Gliding has witnessed four fatalities from medical causes since 1966, all being heart attacks and not one injuring anyone else. Charles Dollfus, who ballooned from Edwardian days to the 1970s, could not recall a single ballooning accident attributable to medical mishap. More recent successors cannot recall such an event from later days. All commercial balloon pilots, whether or not their 'aerial work' involves passengers, must pass full medical examinations (overseen by the Civil Aviation Authority). It is expected that a greater involvement with Europe, and a harder-headed attitude by some states to medicals in general, will increase restrictions in the future, despite a complete lack of evidence impelling such change.

Of the 950 British balloon pilots there are about a third with commercial licences. The remainder are those who fly principally for fun, who take up friends or family, who *do* know who is in the basket with them, who prefer views unframed by armpits, who think that punters push boats with poles, and who dig into their *own* pockets to pay for the pastime which they treasure so deeply.

It may be a touch more costly to finance their sport themselves, but at least they never meet the problem of someone grieving – out loud and vehemently – that a precious box of Kleenex has failed to get on board.

CHAPTER 11

Exotic flying

'I'm not normally a bad loser, but to lose out on $11,000 through sheer incontinence... It's money down the drain.' The blessings, hazards, merits, delights and inconveniences of flying in foreign air.

THIRTY YEARS AGO OR SO, when there was leg-room on aircraft for passengers, when engines had propellers, and only dozens of people were on board each plane instead of hundreds, there was no public address system. The team up front would write flight information on a piece of paper – pilot's name, time of arrival, what was down below, and so forth – before handing this to the front row. It was then passed from row to row, with everyone reassured to learn that Manchester was underneath, the stewardesses were Marjorie and Jennifer, and Gander would be reached in 10 hours' time. One perfidious trick from those days was to keep this paper, save it for another flight (destined, instead, for Beirut or Alexandria) and exchange old news for the new during the next paper round. Consternation was always good to hear, with the pilot – as like as not – forced to leave his paperback and quell anxiety.

It is nice to think that balloonists, traditionally uncertain of their destination, would have been more relaxed than most when encountering this subterfuge. The old Gordon Bennett racers, for example, were often splendidly off-hand in their reports. 'We argued whether it was the Black Sea or the Caspian… Those cattle did look Rumanian… It took us 14 days of walking after our landing to find *anyone*, and then they proved to be Russians!' There is an allure about an unknown destination, whether or not it is known, more or less, where it should be.

Normally in life we tend to follow the beaten track. We follow friends' directions to reach their houses. We obey instructions when we are lost: 'This way to the castle – the beach – the ferry – the re-cycling centre.' We tend not to adventure up roads/tracks leading to 'Farm Only'. We can even resent minor roads, their promise being scanty, their likely perseverance visibly faint-hearted. Much as we begrudge the multi-car, multi-truck, multi-bus and multi-lane race-tracks of the motorways these do exert a magnetism, pulling us from by-ways, discouraging us from exploration, preventing us from intimacy with our countryside.

Everything changes when we have embarked upon a voyage by balloon, with a different set of values then pre-eminent. The spots chosen for landings are not selected for their remoteness but tend to be far from the customary rut (and from motorways). These final destinations are doubly unknown, being quite unknown before we land in them and certainly

For some reason, or for no detectable reason, certain locations have become launch pads for balloons. Chateau d'Oex to the east of Lake Geneva is one such magnet.

141

unknown in that, via ordinary life, we would never get to meet them. Of course they are someone's, or something's, property but – for a time – they are also ours. We feel their grass, regard their trees, admire their views, and receive splendid affirmation that everywhere has some kind of enchantment for visitors to savour. Part of landing's joy is the not-knowingness of it all, the sense of discovery, the brief involvement with some other kind of life in some other kind of place.

This pleasure is increased still further if the flight starts (or ends) in a foreign land. Even foreign grass seems different, as well as foreign fences, crops, trackways, homes, and the people and the talk. Good heavens, but that farmer really *is* wearing clogs! And that dog *did* understand whatever it was he said! As for the tractor which helped with the retrieve, or the drink which helped thereafter, they are not necessarily better than such aids in Britain, but they are different. At the time they therefore seem superior.

It is also easy to regard other countries almost as a playground, particularly for balloonists abruptly landing on a piece of them. Once in France we were experiencing difficulty leaving a field, the only gate being padlocked and no key-owner discoverable despite a lengthy search. 'Pas de problème,' said a policeman, extracting bolt-cutters from his car. Many a foreign setback can disappear with a simplicity unknown in Britain. Contrarily much straightforwardness can be horrendous elsewhere – Shops will be closed 'for a week' owing to the festival – You must pay $100, but 'only with a $100 bill' – You should have '16 passport-sized photos' of yourself 'in colour' – 'No, the machine is broken'. Such impossibilities can instantly vanish if the obstreperous official realises you have the same birthday/come from Manchester/are on your honeymoon. Foreign means different, with differences either better or worse than things back home (and probably more intriguing).

John Deans, writing in the *Aerostat*, expressed, in forthright terms, one aspect of alien voyaging. 'When you have travelled half way round the world the last thing you want to hear are the two words that make the hairs on the back of your neck stand up, and your palms start sweating. They are not the two words British balloonists may use in rude gesticulation. They are simply: NO PROBLEM. These are terrifying and, sure enough, on the first day of the (Manila) event, the organisers informed us that we were not to worry, the balloon was safely in the country,

We are so used to our ground-based living that the world seen from above can seem doubly enchanting, fascinating, more beautiful than ever before, or downright bewildering.

even though it had not been seen. It was with customs who would not release it – but 'please do not worry, there is no problem'.

Taxi is the one word recognisable in every nation. Problem – and no problem – are contenders for second place in this form of global-speak. When requesting a taxi (and hoping to be understood) no guarantee exists about the kind of taxi which will arrive (or when or how). Similarly no notion is ever possible concerning the time and cost (and sweat and tears) before 'no problem' vanishes.

The *Aerostat*, official bi-monthly publication of the British Balloon and Airship Club, favours reports from foreign lands. Or perhaps its contributing balloonists write more frequently of experiences elsewhere. In any case they make absorbing reading, if only for the variety of material thought relevant by these reporters as they savour their remembrances before flavouring their writing as they think fit. They all, in different ways from different places, come under the heading of foreign flying:

'The hotel was on the outskirts of the city, and hot water would be available after June 5, i.e. two weeks after our departure…' *(Moscow)*

'We passed a lot of Frenchmen with guns, who were really nice, and Frenchmen in Peugots who were not…' *(Calais)*

'The only problem occurred when one pilot flying low over the ice met a land yacht…' *(Zell am Zee)*

'Low flying rules were suspended for the duration, with pilots encouraged to touch down in McDonalds' car parks whenever possible…' *(Canberra)*

'"We will land by the tamarisk." What tamarisk?' *(Luxor)*

'Vultures perching in the acacia trees are undisturbed by the intrusion…' *(Maasai Mara)*

'A night at 10,000 feet with torrential rain, barking dogs and just-above-zero temperatures confirmed my belief that I am probably past camping as a method of relaxation…' *(Bhutan)*

'Although only one group was relieved of a money-belt, souvenir hunters frequently helped themselves to anything not welded down…' *(Albania)*

'Rubens had to stop on a tree, holding one of its branches, waiting for the wind to change and push him into an open space in the middle of a banana plantation… Our salvation

Even freeways, motorways and parking lots can have appeal when they and their restrictions are safely down below.

was the kindness of the people – and their ox-carts.' *(Brazil)*

'Animals took no notice, perhaps proving the rule that the more relaxed the farmer, the more relaxed their animals…' *(Burgundy)*

'Fiesta flying in the city permitted many air-to-ground interviews with lovely ladies on their bedroom balconies…' *(St Petersburg)*

'If there's one thing worse than having to be somewhere at 7 am, it's having to be somewhere at 7 am in rain…' *(Ireland)*

'On one launch I noticed a big bulge under my envelope only to find a lady sitting cross-legged sewing repairs… (After landing) we were joined by three village girls who were fascinated with the hairs on our white fore-arms…' *(Beijing)*

'Nick adjusted the front of his dad's Land Cruiser when he slid into the back of a car...' *(Switzerland)*

'Here our launch site was a dried-up river bed...' *(Tunisia)*

'We covered the radios in thick, wooly walking socks which kept them warm enough to work...' *(Arosa)*

'When they get behind the wheel, watch out! Accidents seem rare, but how – I just don't know...' *(South Korea)*

'I'm not normally a bad loser, but to miss out on $11,000 through sheer incontinence!... It's money down the drain...' *(Malaysia)*

'Then there was this termite hill... where did they learn to make concrete?' *(Zimbabwe)*

'We met the others trying to be nice to a policeman who had just pulled them doing 80 mph towing a trailer on a motorway that wasn't open yet...' *(Poland)*

'Rule No. 2 – You must always be sounding your horn (apparently it makes the car go faster)...' *(India)*

'The only real problems are ostriches and, in particular, one Mr Nasty who hated everyone...' *(South Africa)*

'Once airborne, passenger Michael Orr proposed to his girlfriend Susan – She accepted...' *(Ireland)*

'The 8 am briefings came to resemble a war zone as the walking wounded started to appear with various cuts, bruises, plaster casts...' *(Austria)*

'No amount of telling could accurately describe the scene; it really has to be seen to be fully appreciated...' *(Albuquerque)*

I t is appropriate to end these foreign tales on both an up-beat note and from Albuquerque, New Mexico. That particular location hosts quite the most extraordinary balloon gathering of them all, and has done so every year since the first international championships were held there in 1973. The local weather is usually ideal. The surrounding landscape, although well equipped with mountains, a major river and lots of electricity, is rich with landing sites. The city itself is apparently grateful for an invasion of pick-up trucks, mobile homes, 4-wheel drives, campers, and trailers plus, of course, balloonists and all their gear. Other cities could have become 'ballooning capital of the world' but Albuquerque was home to the Cutter family, notably Bill and Sid. They organised the first big-scale aggregation of balloons, and balloons have never gone away, notably during October of each year when ballooning's community knows it is 'Albuquerque time' once more.

The mass ascent is the most extraordinary event of an extraordinary couple of weeks. To be airborne in the company of several *hundred* balloons is to know that about a couple of *thousand* people are equally airborne within, say, two miles. Several jumbo's-worth of individuals are therefore standing there, some within hailing distance, all travelling with the wind, and all ascending and descending in their own sweet time like colourful yo-yos. Great care is necessary in such compression to prevent collision, with the one below not knowing (for sure) what is above, and the one above forced to climb if the one below is gaining in altitude. With these mass ascents there are several hundred *tons* of airborne matter, if the weight of all balloons and their balloonists are combined.

Such a massive influx of balloons might imply that modern aeronauts, like the animals which congregate in herds, are happiest in crowds, but this is only partly true. They do like to be in colossal crowds, *and* in smaller crowds, *and* in single figures, *and* even on their own, perhaps taking off and flying because – quite suddenly – it seemed a perfect evening for taking leave of Earth. Flying from the sprawling development of Albuquerque might also imply that conurbations provide optimum locations for ascension, but this is another form of partial truth. Cities *are* good departure points, but so are village greens, and open fields, and bits of emptiness that suddenly seem suitable for laying out, for inflation, and for taking to the air. The practise of ballooning (notably the hot-air kind) must be the most wide-ranging, the most adaptable, and the least choosy of all adventuring.

It is therefore hard to think of places where balloons have never been involved. They have flown past the pyramids, over Luxor, by the big game herds, across mountain ranges, over deserts, above forests, on lakes, in the clouds, over oceans, and even above the Arctic, starting – for good measure – at 90 North. They fly at (almost) any height, brushing the grasses, flicking through the tree-tops, and being one mile or ten above the ground. There are plans for going higher still, perhaps to 130,000 feet and therefore 24 miles higher than the trees. Balloons are surely not ubiquitous, but do come close.

As for the countries over which they fly there are still lands where a hot-air balloon has not yet been seen, but the number

There is nowhere, however unkempt or casual, that does not appear improved by flying past it in a balloon.

is lessening each and every year. Phil Dunnington and Pete Bish, rivals in this regard, have competed over many years concerning the number of nations they each have below their belt (and have had below their baskets at some time in the past). The current score is 28 for Pete and 63 for Phil, with Phil's unfair advantage being paid to travel plus balloon whereas Pete has some other kind of job.

Back in 1960, when Ed Yost coaxed ONR 1 into the air, and initiated propane flight, gas balloons had been flown here and there around the globe, but the arrival of heated air displaced the difficult need for hydrogen, for coal gas or for costly helium. Without doubt Propane Phil and Butane Bish would not have amassed such formidable totals had they not been blessed with the relative simplicity of full tanks of LPG, with glowing burners, and with light-weight envelopes to get them in the air above, for example, Slovenia, Qatar, Iceland, Estonia, Andorra, Lichtenstein, Antigua, Oman, Bhutan, Thailand, Paraguay, Jordan, Albania, Malta, Nigeria, and Lithuania, as well as most of the more likely nations dotted around the world.

It *is* fun to reach unknown destinations even in one's native land. It is yet more so to reach them in such exotic circumstance, where anything can happen and where it often does. With balloons already over the North Pole and Mount Everest, the Atlantic and Pacific, and with them attempting to fly right round planet Earth, it might seem as if there is nowhere else to go. Of course that is not true, with every balloon flight traversing a route which, in all probability, has *never* been flown before, and with every such adventure therefore a unique experience.

Besides, what are Phil and Pete planning at this very moment? Surely these fierce competitors, humiliating the rest of us, cannot rest at a modest 63? There are, as we can easily suggest, lots and lots of little islands they have not yet added to their list, enabling their fulsome log-books to be suitably embellished before – alas, alas – the land beneath just finishes and both these ardent combatants head directly out to sea.

It is so weird to wander over – anything, breaking all the normal rules for normal travel on the ground.

CHAPTER 12

Hot-air airships

'**I**t would have been nice to have had a bit more right,' says one balloonist when the flight is done. 'Or a bit more left,' says a companion. There is appeal in unknown destinations. There is also a wish, quite frequently, for directional control.

'JOURNEY TO AN UNKNOWN DESTINATION' proclaimed the billboard. I had already learned this most elemental ballooning truth (if not much else) before my first ascent, but had not fully grasped this prime fact of sailing helplessly and inexorably with the wind – until seeing those printed words. Would we really be taking off entirely uncertain of the place of touching down? More to the point was the pilot equally unknowing?

'Not, how you say, foggiest,' replied this Dutchman, casually compounding his sense of ignorance.

Later he inferred we might travel east, and so it happened that we voyaged steadfastly north-west. I shall never forget the destination, just as I have never absolutely forgotten every other touch-down site, but it and all the others were quite unknown beforehand. This blindness is a basic joy for balloonists, but is anathema for other individuals who require more order in their lives. Fate may know (presumably) what location is in store – which tree, what field, which asylum (it has been known) or what cemetery (crudely premature) – but a pilot has no such prescience. He is probably wrong when expressing an opinion a mere five minutes before he (and his companions) become re-united with the earth. That uncertainty, even at the eleventh hour, is a principal pleasure of this form of flight.

Nevertheless there are occasions when steerage could be a boon. How awful it was to land in that mire, and to smell unpardonably for several hours thereafter, merely because the nearby grassy field had abruptly proved impossible. And where did the gust come from which suddenly turned an expected car-park landing (concrete, open space, no problem) into one *within* the open back (metal, confinement, big problem) of one parked truck, a vehicle which promptly started travelling on its four wheels, with every kind of possibility then ahead – that plate-glass window, those lamp-posts, an irrigation ditch? In fact it merely hit a car.

There have been – in everyone's experience – many moments which were partnered by a desperate longing for more control, for just one iota more control. Dry-stone walls, hawthorn hedges or sewage systems can make even the most dedicated balloonist long for guidance greater than a balloon is able to provide.

'Could have done with a bit more left,' says the pilot afterwards, removing himself from some entanglement.

'Or a bit more right,' says a companion, while wondering

They are large. They can be ungainly. They are also more costly than the average balloon, but they can be steered and even return to the place they started from.

what magnetism it is which pulls balloons towards the only obstacles in view. The thought of steering, despite the joy of unknown destinations, does – at times – have considerable appeal.

Thus it happened that planning began by a group of us to build a hot-air airship. The year was 1964. The gas balloon safari over Africa had been successfully concluded, but had been tinged with regret – quite frequently – that we could not have been, say, a mile to the east and over that herd rather than within a forest of fever trees, the kind with lengthy spines. This horizontal failing was partnered by an inability to fly at the most convenient altitude. A gas balloon, such as we employed, is not a device which can always be persuaded to fly at a chosen height. A handful of sand too many may, when jettisoned overboard, send the balloonist much too high. A compensatory pull on the valve line may then diminish that gain too much, causing a leap-frog form of flight. In short, during our time in Africa, we had often been at the wrong height and over the wrong place far too frequently.

Shortly after our return to the United Kingdom, enthusiastic for the theory of ballooning if not its actuality, the channel of water separating it from France was successfully crossed by the Raven 'Vulcoon' team. A brand new age for hot air flight had decidedly arrived and, judging by the flight path of the cross-Channel event, it would be an age with rather more control than is feasible with gas. Nine months after that Raven success, when work took me to America, I stopped off at Sioux Falls in South Dakota. From there Don Piccard gave me a flight in what by then was named the Channel Champ, and we sailed one freezing day over rock-hard fields which had been corn. For a gas balloonist, whose valving of gas and jettisoning of sand had provided only modest altitude control, it was astonishing to travel low over fields and then *ascend* to jump each fence. Don immodestly exclaimed that he preferred golf fairways where *real* low flying could be achieved.

'The greens are better still,' he added jauntily, never averse to a touch or two of showmanship.

Despite the rhetoric it was plain that controlled jets of propane could be more precisely influential over height than shovelfuls of sand could ever be, and I was entranced. If an engine and a rudder could be added to control direction the possibilities of a hot-air airship were doubly captivating, with both horizontal *and* vertical control a dual possibility.

Upon my return to England work began at once (and that was part, if not most, of our undoing). Within one week I and Malcolm Brighton (in particular) were buying fabric – a thousand square yards of it. We bought a 1,600cc Volkswagen engine, plus a propeller to go with it. And we decided to create our own propane burner rather than copy the American design. There is nothing quite like unbridled enthusiasm for getting things done. There is also nothing quite like a newcomer's conceit for turning ignorance into confidence, for thinking that energy liberally applied will conquer everything.

This development of a heating system added to the general sense of buoyancy. Instead of mimicking Raven's three burners, each of these surrounded by a coiled inlet pipe, we elected to have one bigger unit. 'Saves on weight, tubing and money,' we chortled, deriding the South Dakotan way (which had succeeded brilliantly). Our piping coils formed a burner one foot in diameter, and we lit its four propane nozzles when everything had been properly connected. The resultant flame looked great; so we increased the flow. This magnificent flame then gradually ascended before vanishing off the top, leaving us with four fountains of unlit propane, along with total astonishment on our faces.

'Flames can't just go out,' we uttered, having just seen them do so.

'Oh yes they can', said a knowledgeable friend; 'You've got your nozzle speed in excess of your flame speed. What you need is a spoiler, something to slow down the nozzle velocity.'

Such a reply should have dented our arrogance dramatically, but the quaint event – and explanation – merely stiffened our resolve to get things done our way. We promptly located all manner of spoilers, of things to reduce that propane flow, and none worked so splendidly as a plastering-trowel. When placed above one squirting nozzle it held the flame in place. With four such trowels, these speedily purchased, we had a perfect burner. Or rather we had a burner which did not extinguish its flame if asked to burn more brightly.

'Weld these together,' we instructed a nearby garage friend, and we later revelled – like the flame – in our joint brilliance.

As for the airship we called it *Wasp*, with alternating black and yellow fabric bands to emphasise the name of our Warm Air Ship Project. Its gondola was more akin to a rubber boat and,

Advertisers like them because, unlike balloons which travel inexorably downwind, they can hover or circle to ensure their messages are hammered home.

via the VW engine with its shiny propeller, we drove it at great speed around a nearby lake. For trial inflations we planned to use a local sandpit, this being deep and therefore protected from all wind. We considered its sandy base most congenial, for screwing in anchor points, for providing instant ballast. Within an extraordinarily short time, a few weeks rather than months, we were ready to coerce heated air into our 80,000 cubic feet of envelope. In no time at all, or so we figured, everything would be ready for flight trials over Greenland, our chosen destination. How splendid it would be to ascend over teeming millions of seabirds, or sea mammals, and forever *steering* where we wished to go.

Cliches can be so miserably valid: we were tremendously proud and then we fell, ever so emphatically. The first problem, dubbed sloosh, arose when hot air merrily cavorted either to the ship's front end or to its rear. We tried baffles, rodding poles, and inflatable tubes (or all three in unison), but still the sloosh confounded us – mainly for the reason that our craft, too speedily designed, had an insufficiently rounded upper surface. This single error led on to others. While attempting to cure that fore-or-aft behaviour we pumped in too much heat, thereby helping to destroy the fabric's coating. Then, as heated air seeped through the fabric, we heated yet more air to try to gain more lift.

Soon we had 1,000 square yards of porous material, incapable of containing air, and we also had far less useful money in the bank. We shook our heads more wisely now, but too belatedly. Thenceforth the Greenland fauna swam or flew in unmolested style, and a man from Farnborough gained all those black and yellow yards for the price of six pounds ten. *Wasp's* death was formally announced in 1966, and our group unhappily retired to lick its wounds, mainly by seeking employment which actually paid us for our work.

Nevertheless failure has its place in progress. Other individuals could see our errors, and were perhaps stimulated by them. It is necessary for someone to put feet upon a ladder's first rung, and then probably to fail, causing someone else to think of a better way of achieving the all-important second rung. That further step may also lead to failure, with every form of pioneering such a chancy business. Yet another person may then be first to achieve the third rung, and possibly gain the desired success. Very few pioneers triumph at their first attempt, these earliest of individuals not necessarily practical, or even

The behemoths can be surprisingly controllable, with markers dropped within millimetres of the aiming point.

competent, but they are emphatic dreamers. They are possibly a bit remote from normal rules and practicalities in order to have their dreams. The later individuals, more worldly-wise, more competent technically, and better able to summon financial aid, are not of the dreamy kind. Nevertheless they watch the earlier antics, and then they build upon them.

Anyone who doubts this generality should look, for example, at photographs of early flying machines, and then be amazed at the hopelessness of almost all of them. In no way could 99 per cent of the flapping, leaping, multi-winged, under-powered and over-weight devices *ever* have become airborne, but each were promoted with as much vigour, and time, and cash, and courage, as those which did succeed in taking to the air. Dreamers dream, and possibly inspire. Others watch as the dreams take curious shape, pathetically, frighteningly and (probably) catastrophically. The others then do rather better, and may even make the dreamers' dreams come true.

Original pioneers can believe that, without their earlier efforts, the successors would never have embarked upon their work, and then succeeded. This has to be untrue. There would have been balloons whether or not two brothers from Annonay had started tinkering, wrong-headedly, with smoke. There would have been aviation without two bicycle manufacturers attaching an engine to two propellers and two pairs of wings. The pioneers pioneer, successfully or not, but there is (generally) an inevitability about their wishes coming true. If they fail – to make a better mouse-trap – someone else will do so within a year or two.

The notion of a steerable balloon has always had appeal. It was first expressed very shortly after the earliest ascents, with subsequent aerostats carrying sails, oars, and rudders to help them navigate. Unfortunately, with any free-flying balloon, these extras can do nothing of the sort. The balloons not only had to lose their spherical outline but be given mechanical propulsion before, as airships, they could travel anywhere – instead of inexorably downwind. When these dirigibles (steerables) did arise they were inflated with gas, there being – in the early days – no sane method for filling them with heated air. *Wasp* had tried, and *Wasp* had failed. It was up to someone else to make the hot-air notion work.

On 6 January 1973, a cold easterly wind was blowing over southern England. Visibility was poor and cloud base was barely higher than the ground. An event, to be known – with good

155

reason – as the Icicle Meet, had been scheduled for that initial weekend of the new year. A few balloons did manage to fly, such as *Bristol Belle*, Britain's first home-grown propane-fired balloon, and everyone hoped better conditions would prevail on the following day. Dick Wirth and Tom Donnelly, in particular, were hoping things would go well for *Jumpin' Jack Flash*, the earliest creation from their brand-new Thunder company.

Then, from behind the trees and brilliantly stage-managed, arose a shape, the like of which had never been seen before. Don Cameron and Teddy Hall were at the controls of G-BAMK, the world's first hot-air airship. Only seven years had passed since *Wasp* had been abandoned, its 80,000 cubic feet having never left the ground, and suddenly there was this successor, lumbering noisily through the sky. The object was not handsome, with stress lines all too visible where the load was greatest. It was also none too nimble, making heavy weather of a circuit around the take-off field, but it was assuredly being steered and was also, most positively, flying through the air. When eventually it had been turned to point directly into wind its huge shape not only approached the delighted crowd of onlookers but descended simultaneously. It landed to great applause, and Page 1 of *The Times* celebrated this great achievement on the following day with a splendid photograph. The hot-air airship had arrived.

In theory such a craft has great potential. It can go where its pilot wishes it to go. It can also hover, this stationary ability being a boon for advertisers. It can fly more cheaply than any helicopter could ever do and, at the day's end, can be packed away – save for the gondola – much like a balloon. Unfortunately it will always be big. As we with *Wasp* had realised, after seeing its many thousands of cubic feet above the ground (if not flying through the air), there is an awful lot of hot-air airship to be propelled. Bulk does not greatly matter with an ordinary balloon. If twice the size, so what, save at the landing field when there is twice the mass to be halted as it cavorts across the land.

Bulk matters greatly when an object must be shoved through the air (as opposed to floating with it). Bulk matters even more when the shoving is done at speed, with drag proportional not only to the airship's diameter but to the square of its velocity. With more than four times the power necessary to increase speed from, say, 10 miles an hour to 20 miles an hour the awesome diameter of a fat airship puts haste firmly to one side.

A few of them cruising, as in Switzerland, can 'seemingly occupy one entire valley when several are in the air at once'.

The things are therefore slow. And ponderous. And fair weather fliers. And quite expensive. And therefore not the total delight originally imagined when notions of steering a balloon first came to mind.

Nevertheless they have their devotees. They also have their competitions where the talk, although different, brings back memories of 'nationals' and 'worlds' during which balloons and their balloonists strive to beat each other.

'Two bullseyes and three pools must be done clockwise,' states the competitions director; 'That's after a 26 k cross-country, but take your markers as the starting gate will be open at 7.15.'

This particular briefing, far briefer than normal, was given at Besancon, France, during the 3rd World Hot-Air Airship Championship held in 1992. There were 14 entrants, these crews arriving from Japan, USA, Brazil, UK, Sweden, Germany, Switzerland, and France. It followed similar championships, at Luxembourg in 1988 and Nottingham in 1990. Besancon was chosen for the third venue partly because it had been the first European city to 'use an airship for promotional purposes' and was happy to be host to the variety of airships assembling to fly around, and compete nearby, the 'greenest' city in France.

The event was not without incident. Petersen of Germany ceased being favourite when his Rotax engine gave up with a leak in the cooling system. Rick Wallace, of America, crashed his craft into a football-field floodlight mast. The Swiss lent him their old envelope, but this split at the first inflation. The Adler ship (from Germany) burst during the launch for the fifth flight, and Tom Sage of Britain had to withdraw after injuring his right arm. Attrition was cutting swathes, but the show went on in the noblest spirit of competitive airshipping. It is not the winning nor the taking part which matters, but the surviving long enough to take part. In the end it was well-moustached Guy Moyano from Luxembourg who achieved the handsome trophy, having coaxed his Cameron-built *Lux-Post* ship nearer bullseyes, pools, and touch-and-gos than anyone else.

Next major competitive stop was Chateau d'Oex in Switzerland for the 1994 event when 16 craft from eight nations gathered to compete. This too was eventful, with the American Wallace again having trouble (with a broken pressurisation fan), with Besnard of France encountering power lines (blacking out houses *and* earning penalty points), with Taucher of Germany

Balloons can be revolved, via their turning vents, enabling their messages to face the crowd, but they cannot hover as hot-air airships can, and do.

suffering a fuel blockage, with Contegiacomo of Italy losing his map (sucked into the propeller to be spewed out as confetti) and Moyano of Luxembourg, the former winner, experiencing less intriguing engine problems. Rather like the annual London-Brighton veteran car run much of hot-air airship fun must be in fixing repairs before the time runs out.

There is a degree of finesse to this airship business not always apparent in the ballooning competitions. The leviathans may look colossal, and seemingly occupy one entire valley when several are in the air hurtling along at some 15 miles an hour, but the degree of control can be magnificent. At Valle d'Aosta, for the 5th World Championships, Tom Sage of Britain thought he had done well when placing his marker only 75 *milli*metres from the centre of the bull. Indeed he had done well, but he had only gained 6th position. The actual winner, with the refinement of a triple-20 darts player, had dropped his marker 5 mm from the centre, while the best runners-up were 6, 7 and 8 mm from the middle of that bull. Mere balloonists would be happy, very, very happy, if their marker fell 5 metres from a chosen spot, or one thousand times as far.

H ot-air airships have improved, in appearance, in speed and manoeuvrability, since that debut at Marsh Benham Farm in 1973. A major step forward occurred when pressurisation was first contrived. Normal pressure airships, filled with gas and equipped with ballonets (to maintain internal volume whether ascending or descending), are only serviceable because the pressure within the envelope is fractionally greater than the ambient pressure. This differential is less than 1 per cent but, as rigidity is a function both of pressure and of diameter, the huge bulk of pressure airships (sometimes known as blimps) is sufficient to give them the firmness that they need.

So too with hot-air airships. The attachment of fins, for example, and the working of control surfaces, become much easier when the envelope is firm. (Or at least firmer than it would be without pressure difference.) This difference is easier to acquire with gas airships, as the gas container can readily be sealed. The mass of hot air within a hot-air airship cannot be enclosed in similar fashion, as it must constantly be heated to offset the inevitable loss of warmth. Nevertheless, with clever designs incorporating fans, this has been achieved, and the resultant airships look better, fly better and are more controllable.

As might be expected they are harder to inflate than hot air balloons. David Fish, a balloonist, learned this truth when wishing to broaden his experience and acquire airship expertise. In the *Aerostat* (of June 1994) he summed up the necessary procedure:

'Before the envelope is connected, both engines are run up and a burner check is completed. The envelope is attached to the gondola by four V shackles. There is a nose line which... can be tied off to a vehicle. The fin and internal rigging (need) checking to prevent them becoming entangled during inflation... The pressurising engine... is used to inflate the ship, and the parachute... is located into position... The ship is brought upright by tilting the burner over... the crew must balance the nose and tail to keep them level... Once upright the main engine is run... and the rudder is checked to make sure it works correctly...'.

With the engine running, the burner firing, and a pressurisation fan busily maintaining the airship's proper shape, all is set to go. The huge shape can then be coaxed into take-off, and the rudder brought into play so that the ship can demonstrate its fundamental difference from all balloons by going elsewhere than downwind. At least, in theory, that is what they do.

It so happened that another Icicle Meet witnessed the most spectacular failure of a hot-air airship to manoeuvre properly. The meet of 1973 had welcomed the first public demonstration of such a craft. The meet of 1994 witnessed, no less publicly, the awesome inability of a similar device to circumnavigate a tree. The former *Zanussi* airship, crudely re-named when both the Z and the second S were encouraged to disappear, then became *US 1* after further encouragement. It had been brought to the Icicle gathering as one more item for display.

Phil Dunnington and Malcolm White were to be the pilots. It took off well enough, and Phil later told the tale. 'We initiated a right turn, with the intention of staying low, then left rudder to maintain position – but nothing happened. The airship started to drift towards a downwind tree. Malcolm burned and burned, but the airship didn't climb enough to clear the tree, and we couldn't steer to avoid it. We were about 80 feet up at this time, and considered an emergency landing, but facing forward in an airship is the worst possible way, and you are without the comfort of all-forgiving wicker to take the impact.'

Having hit the tree 'only 10 feet beneath its crown' they quickly became embedded in its canopy. As the airship deflated its gondola began to tip. The wind was also picking up, threatening to send both men towards the ground. 'It was very frightening,' reported Phil, most understandably (even if he has stated he is only truly scared when above 3,000 feet). The arrival of the fire-brigade enabled Phil and Malcolm to reach the ground, but the airship could not be so easily disentangled from the tree. G-BEPZ ended its life there and then, with the surviving bits and pieces headed for retirement at the British Balloon Museum and Library, recipient of many an ancient aerostat.

Perhaps hot-air airships will find a role – one day. They do exist. They have improved. They do fly well over relatively wind-free areas. And their numbers are increasing, but only slowly. When hot-air balloons were also in their infancy they too were frequently involved with forestry, and with the need for almost zero-wind. Since those earliest days they have advanced year by year – better fabrics, better deflation designs, more efficient dumping systems, turning vents, flexi-rigid poles, scoops, stouter baskets, multiple burners – so that encounters with land-based items are less probable. There has not been such inducement, as has been engendered by the tremendous market for hot-air balloons, to progress with the hot-air airship kind.

But if the dirigible market were suddenly to increase, if hot-air airships became the mainstay of ballooning manufacturers, the craft might leap ahead in their capabilities. Who knows, but one kind might prove to be the very thing for floating over the teeming million of seabirds, the schools of spouting mammals, that flourish so excitingly off and on the coast of Greenland. Now there is a great idea!

CHAPTER 13

Models
and ballooniana

Ever since their start, the man-carrying balloons have spawned other industries, all related to but distant from the prime endeavour. The balloon motif, used for decoration from the very beginning, is still employed, and miniature balloons, also with an ancient history, are more in vogue than ever before.

THE MAN WAS PUFFING UP THE SLOPE at Bristol's Ashton Court. Balloons were being inflated by the top of the hill, and he was plainly intending to join the crowd. As drawback, causing most of the puffing, he was carrying his entire balloon. As further disadvantage he was quite the oldest person to be seen that day, but he still had breath to spare.

'If you've got to go,' he said, 'I can't think of a better way.'

With that Charles Saffery carried on towards his goal. He does indeed have many years beneath his belt, and he did that day have a balloon draped about him, but his load was what he calls a mini-balloon. He, more than anyone else, has promoted this form of aerostation and has been promoting it since 1929. Hills, and lungs, permitting, he has no intention of giving up the sport.

An older brother had helped to serve as inspiration. Being a member of the Royal Aero Club (then in Piccadilly) the young Charles was able to see 'the most beautiful pictures of the first balloons'. These fired the 14-year-old's imagination. So too the exploits of his older brother, one of a flying fraternity learning to advance their trade at Stag Lane aerodrome. Their favoured stunt was to 'bounce' a biplane off the rounded top of a gas works, with the authorities 'rather cross' in consequence. Young Charles was given flights but (understandably) would later concentrate his energies upon model flying, notably of aerostats.

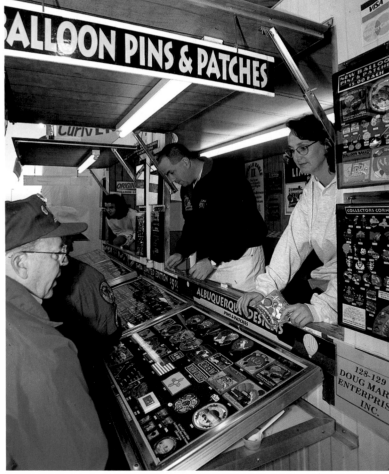

Ballooning is undoubtedly an ancient pastime, being the earliest form of aviation. Model ballooning – without the benefit/drawback of human passengers – has an even longer history, with miniature versions being the oldest form of free flying device. They enabled, for example, the famous Montgolfier brothers to test their theories. One year before the Montgolfier-inspired and manned ascent from Paris the brothers had heated the air within a silken envelope. This earliest of their prototypes had floated to reach the ceiling. Their second balloon, made from paper, allegedly ascended to 600 feet. Thus encouraged they built a third (of 22,000 cubic feet) and it departed from the square at Annonay to land 10 minutes later, having possibly travelled higher still.

As soon as news of this astonishment had reached France's capital its Paris Academy was stirred into competition. This institution, jealous of such provincial pioneering, promptly instructed the 37-year-old physicist, Jacques Charles, to build a

You name it, you've got it. You think of it, you do it. Everything is variations upon a theme, and it is all on show whenever and wherever the bigger brethren are performing.

hydrogen balloon, this lightest of gases having been discovered only 17 years earlier. Professor Charles immediately set to work, ably assisted by two brothers of the Robert family. Their prototype device, when completed, was 12 ft in diameter. It weighed 25 lb and had an internal capacity of 943 cubic feet. Precisely 498 lb of acid and 1,000 lb of iron were then used to fill it with gas, and on 27 August 1783 it flew from the Champ de Mars to land 15 miles away. This entirely successful flight of a model balloon had lasted 45 minutes.

Following this double experimentation, with both gas and hot air models, the scene was therefore set for the two manned ascents which took place in November (hot air) and December (gas) of that year. Models were also to show the way in Britain for Britain's first home-grown aeronauts. James Sadler, later to become the first English-born balloon pilot, released a 30-ft balloon from the gardens of Queen's College, Oxford, on 9 February 1784 (and he later flew on 4 October of that same year, also from Oxford). The very first Briton to fly (as usually accredited) was James Tytler of Edinburgh. He too started with a trial balloon. This went up on 12 March (and therefore a few weeks after Sadler's) but Tytler himself became airborne, even if erratically, on the 25 August and again on 1 September, thereby preceding Sadler's earliest ascent. (Sadler continued with ballooning, most successfully, but Tytler's subsequent efforts were all disastrous.)

Such miniatures are still, on occasion, useful experimentally for manufacturers but, in the main, they are built and operated entirely for their own sake. Those flown by Charles Saffery and others tend to be 200-250 cubic feet in volume, and therefore some 8 ft in diameter. They do not transport a burner into the air (for tedious reasons associated with insurance, possible downwind conflagration, etc.) and therefore fly on the capital of hot air with which they are released. Inevitably they will descend – in time. If the launchers estimate that this time may take their windborne models out of reach/across the river/into those houses they can attach a string and walk/run/gallop with their balloons to enforce descent when need be. The breaking strain of the line should be 100 lbs or so, and a piece of elastic making up part of the line damps out sudden jerks.

There is a charm about these mini-balloons, hugely abundant when their owners assemble for their 'mini-meets'. To quote from Saffery's manual on the subject (co-authored by Nigel Ponsford) the first such gathering occurred at Marsh Benham on 8 January 1978 'when no less than six balloons' were inflated. These were '*Odyssey, Firefly, Hot Plastic, Beeze I, Beeze II,* and *Sally*'. Not only did they all fly but 'history was made when the

first aerial balloon rescue was pulled off by Pete Bish'. Flying tethered in a standard balloon 'he plucked *Beeze II* from the arms of the tree which had attacked it'. One year later, when the number of gathered minis had risen from six to eight, *The English Lady* distinguished herself by 'breaking free on her very first inflation and causing some consternation'. No wonder! Whatever will happen next?

All such balloons, whether undisciplined or not, must be of a certain size to have much chance of becoming airborne. A balloon 8 feet in diameter will have an area of 202 square feet and a volume of 267 cubic feet. This better proportion – of surface area to internal volume – enables a stronger/heavier envelope to be used. If the model is 12 feet in diameter its two equivalent figures are 452 square feet and 903 cubic feet. With such a capacity there is considerable lift available for envelope material, for banners, for anything else intended to be airborne. (With these figures in mind it is convenient to remember that many small balloons capable of carrying a man have diameters of 37 feet, surface areas of 4,300 square feet – assuming they are spherical – and therefore volumes of 26,500 cubic feet.)

Those of us who have attempted the manufacture of extremely modest models, fashioned with tissue paper, Sellotape, cotton and glue, do at least learn that a nasty mis-shapen thing, glueing everything it touches, brings discredit to all concerned, particularly if it publicises its ugliness by becoming airborne. There has to be a better way; indeed there does – and is. Saffery's instructions (in his manual) are all formidable, demeaning and extremely thorough. They may deter the faint-hearted, but the faint-hearted will continue with horrendous, distorted resemblances to last year's garbage sacks. As for the stalwarts who are more determined Saffery's words are clear, concise and vital (for example, in his instructions for a 4.5 ft diameter balloon).

'Proceed as follows –
Make a template of the half gore shape. The angle at the crown will be 180 degrees divided by the number of gores, in this case six, i.e. 30 degrees. The maximum width will be half the circumference, divided by the number of gores; i.e. 7.05 minus 6 equals 1.175, plus a seam allowance of, say, 0.08 feet. The total width of the template, at its widest point, is 1.255 feet. The length of the template will be half the circumference...'.

And that is only half way through the first of his 14 stage-by-stage instructions.

At the top of the same page, by way of (modest) encouragement, is a photograph of Dave Holland holding a fine-looking tissue paper model named *Bengy*. According to the caption 'this material is cheap, but fire and water resistance is low, and this balloon succumbed to the latter'. Poor *Bengy*! Poor Dave Holland, after all those hours with template, gores, seam allowances, and 14 stages of instruction, to see his fine creation succumb to damp.

He was thereby prevented, one presumes, from taking part in that day's competition, these contests often held at the mini-meets. They should, says Saffery, 'cover both the making of the

balloon 4 ft in diameter will have a surface area of 50 square feet and a volume of 33 cubic feet. Such a large area relative to volume means that the device will only fly if made extremely lightly, perhaps with tissue paper as envelope material. A

Mini-balloons can seem as good as the real thing (or better than the real thing, say their promoters). Kermit the Frog doing his thing.

balloon and the owner's skill in flying it'. There are several categories:

Concours d'Elégance
The judges inspect the standard of workmanship, and ease of inflation. (Maximum of 50 points.)

Spot Landing
A large 'X' is marked downwind, and the balloon which touches down nearest to it is adjudged the winner. (Maximum of 25 points for a direct hit, minus 1 point for each yard distant.)

Innovation
For encouragement of new ideas, examples being a flour bomb mechanism, teddy bears parachuting out of the gondola, or rip-stop panels that work after a pre-determined time. (15 points.)

Mass Lift Off
Every participant in such an event gains (10) extra points.

There are other possibilities which spring to mind, writes Saffery, before concluding sternly, 'but remember – safety must be the first consideration.'

The law is involved in mini-ballooning. All aircraft have to be registered (in Britain) with the Civil Aviation Authority. Each is given a number – G-???? – which must be marked on the aircraft. As mini-balloons are a form of aircraft (however distant from 747s) they have therefore become involved with this

'The gathering of ballooniana, pursued to a slight degree by every aeronaut' is as delightful an occupation as attempting to coax the lesser craft to join the sky.

general piece of legislation. Exemptions apply only to those aerostats measuring less than 2 metres wide or high, and to those flown on a tether less than 60 metres long.

With the sudden popularity of mini-balloons, starting in the 1970s, the demand for lawful registration rose considerably. The CAA therefore decided that, as from 1 January 1982, these small balloons would not be part of the *general* register. Instead they would have their own G-FY?? series, but this alteration did nothing to diminish the obligatory demand for registration, and requests still surged towards the CAA. It was therefore decided that, as from May 1983, only those unmanned balloons

Everything a balloonist needs to achieve hot-air flight, save for the balloonist. Many a model is as sophisticated – or more so – as the real thing.

weighing more than 5 kg needed to be registered. The sigh of relief was considerable, not least at the CAA.

Model balloons may have been flying (officially and with documentary evidence) since 1783, but they are still subject to improvement and advance. A high density polythene, one quarter the weight of nylon, has brought down size, with even an indoor model, two feet in diameter, being contrived. Unfortunately the plastic at the mouth tended to melt (during the heating process). Therefore a 'hybrid' version was developed, with a nylon mouth and a polythene remainder. The 'next advance', as reported in the *Aerostat*, was a tube-feed heating system. The burner 'was attached to 100 feet of very light PVC tubing, one quarter of an inch in diameter, and controlled from a propane bottle on the ground'. Thereby 'absolute safety' was combined with a 'realistic look'. The recent

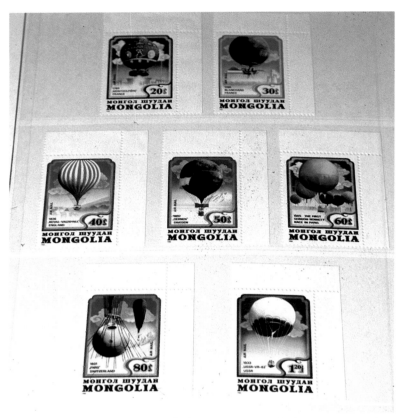

improvements gave 'a possible range of models any size from 2 to 18 feet diameter'. Models may now be deep in their third century of achievement but are still, it would seem, in the developmental phase.

It is difficult not to be enchanted by the major enthusiasm for mini-balloons, despite a preference – by most fliers – for the larger variety. Charles Saffery did reach the top of the hill at Ashton Court that day. He did notice that other people were ascending in baskets on every side of him, but he steadfastly confined all his attention to his own device which, eventually and gracefully, rose into the air. He therefore merits the last word on the subject, on his subject, particularly when he reflects on *his* earlier days, now quite a while ago.

'We were very young, and in retrospect, a bit irresponsible. We gave no thought to the risk of fire, or to insurance claims. We were making paper hot air balloons in the traditional way, with wire stretched across the mouth, on to which was fixed a pad of cotton wool soaked in methylated spirit, and we had the bright idea of embedding the heart of a Roman Candle

firework in the centre of the cotton wool. On one occasion we chased a successful version across Surrey in an open Morris Cowley. At dusk the firework ignited with great effect! The balloon survived, and flew on into the night. Perhaps the lucky boy who found it the next day is still living.'

Or perhaps not, as it was a while ago, but at least there was not another Roman Candle on board to shower him with sparks, also to great effect. Morris Cowleys, meths, cotton wool, and Roman Candles – these smack of different days. Squibs, penny dreadfuls, conkers, bottles of pop, and pistols with caps were probably part and parcel of the scene, but at least the mini-balloons are still flying, and – with Charles Saffery at the helm – more abundantly even than before.

And perhaps, without their airborne furnaces, more safely too.

Whereas mini-ballooning can teach about their bigger brethren, and is therefore educational as well as fun, the collecting of balloon memorabilia can also inform as well as entertain. When the first balloons ascended their success was immediately followed by a tremendous outpouring of balloon designs on practically everything. Fans, tiles, plates, cups, bowls, mugs, door knobs, and of course paintings, etchings and illustrations were besieged by the balloon motif, as if the world had been longing for a new design to come its way. These shapes and outlines were presumably incorporated because they possessed a general appeal, with the obsession for balloons and ballooning extending far beyond artists' studios.

There *was* widespread amazement that flight had been achieved. There was, in consequence, a willingness for this fact to be carved, drawn, and painted on countless artefacts, instant reminders that a brand new age had come to pass. It is more amazing that, in all the years since then, these reminders have never wholly gone away. The motif is still exploited, on cups, on mugs, beer-cans, scarves, table mats, fire-screens, and seemingly everything in need of suitable embellishment to help the thing to sell. A collector of ballooniana can therefore gather objects from any year since 1783, much as stamp-collectors can be equally wide-ranging for all the time since penny postage arrived in 1840. (Great Britain, incidentally, is believed to be the only country *never* to have had balloons upon its postage stamps.)

Illustrations of the earliest ballooning favoured either the 'grand ascension' or any awful aftermath. Each ascent depicted (in general) not only the 'globe aerostatique' but an extremely fashionable array of witnesses to the great event. Each flight's conclusion was not favoured as suitable material unless it ended dangerously, as – for example – 'The Preservation of Sir Richard McGuire who fell into the sea on May 12th 1785', this army officer knighted as a consequence of the pluck and spirit he had shown. Madame Blanchard's fatal descent from Parisian roof-tops in 1819 (after fireworks had ignited her balloon) was always popular, as was Robert Cocking's 'frightful', 'fearful', 'dismal' failure to parachute successfully 18 years later. Major John Money, military aeronaut, made several flights (and later wrote a treatise on ballooning) but his solo flight from Norwich which ended 'in a perilous situation' off Yarmouth is the one most selected by lithographers, painters and water-colourists, with the (temporarily) unfortunate officer beset by ropes and waves as, with a most relaxed countenance, he awaits the distant boats.

Such illustrations not only recorded the spectacle of

'Look at me, I'm a balloonist', 'Look at my collection, I'm a balloonist'. Ballooniana – of all kinds – is part and parcel of the scene.

ballooning, whether good or bad, but the scientific lessons to be learned from humankind's sudden ability to fly. By no means were these accounts always accurate. 'Mr Martyn' was quick off the mark in November 1783, and perhaps a touch too quick, as he plainly had not grasped the facts of flight correctly. His balloon design, more of a boat than an aerostat, had a rudder, several sails, a mast of rope and even a grappling iron to be lowered 'in order that descent can be enforced'. Illustrators were also quick to mock the new invention, as with three gentlemen sitting upon a 'dirigible' of a fish that could not possibly have ascended, let alone 'voyaged' through the air.

Accuracy was never a prerequisite. Robert Cocking, whose 'fatal descent' earned more fame than he ever had in life, did indeed die dramatically aged 61 but, according to illustrators, had either a full head of hair or its empty opposite. Vincent Lunardi changes his appearance in a manner guaranteeing that no one could ever have recognised him in the street, an obscurity not partnering our well-known (and much televised) heroes of today. Almost every aeronaut, according to illustrators, waved a flag of such huge dimensions after take-off that the strength of every aviator must have been phenomenal.

Balloon arrival also meant that artists, notably those clever with altering perspective, could depict aerial views of famous cities. Imaginative and bird's eye views had always been possible, but the fact of human flight created a sudden wealth of panoramas, as if artists had been busily sketching while over

Harold Roxbee Cox, aka Lord Kings Norton, born before the Wrights flew and in aviation all his life, amassed Britain's best collection of l.t.a. memorabilia.

Paris (a popular subject) or Dieppe or any conurbation with potential purchasers residing down below. Balloons were also drawn to fill up space in skies, instead of clouds (always difficult) or birds (standard favourites).

One way and another, for decoration, or journalism, or history, or for the hell of it, the existence of balloons did lead to tremendous quantities of ballooniana. In 1962 Colonel Rupert Preston, then secretary of the Royal Aero Club, sold 221 lots (at Sotheby's) of 'ballooning and aeronautical prints and drawings' which he had amassed to make an impressive collection. Quite a few of these were acquired by Harold Roxbee Cox (later Lord Kings Norton) whose home at Chipping Campden housed (before his death in December 1997) quite the most formidable assortment of balloon memorabilia ever to be gathered under one roof. No indoor wall of that ancient home remained with space unoccupied, no stairway, no shelf, no cupboard, no doorway or door, among the many rooms and passageways dedicated to this man's intelligent gathering of anything and everything concerning what, once upon a time, were called aerostatic globes.

Ballooning is a delightful, intriguing, and thought-provoking pastime. The gathering of ballooniana, pursued to a slight degree by every aeronaut, is also delightful, intriguing and thought-provoking. These two occupations, the flying and the gathering, do most conveniently mesh together, each addictive to all those happy to be embraced by the pair of them.

CHAPTER **14**

The record breakers

'**W**ith human beings the competitive, thrusting and glory-seeking lot they are, it was not long before the mere act of ascension became compounded by the distance travelled, the height achieved, and the endurance of each flight.'

THE VERY FIRST BALLOON ASCENT certainly astonished all Parisians, and then countless others as news of an 'ascension' reverberated around the world. No one seemed to care how far the aeronauts had travelled or how high they had reached; the ascent had been sufficient for amazement, with a pair of courageous individuals going up who did not immediately come down. They had left the ground, had looked upon the world beneath them, and then had landed (alive) to tell the tale. It was more than astonishing, it was magnificent. In fact, coupling both words, the Gentleman's Magazine (of England) called it 'infinitely the most magnificent and most astonishing discovery made… perhaps since the creation'.

Who cared therefore about details, such as distance, height, or time involved? One might as well enquire about the clothing of these pioneers, their footwear, or the colour of their hair. It was more than adequate to know they had been 'embraced by the bosom of the air' (a popular phrase) for their 'wonderous enterprize' (yet another). 'Let posterity know, and knowing be astonished…', as was inscribed on a monument after the first English flight. Astonishment at the ascent was more than ample.

Nevertheless, with human beings the competitive, thrusting and glory-seeking lot they are, it was not long before the mere fact of ascension became compounded by the distance travelled, the height achieved and the endurance of each flight. Less than 14 months after that most magnificent astonishment two men managed to fly across the English Channel, thus achieving the first international sortie as well as the first sea-crossing. Their distance flown was some 35 miles (as they landed '12 miles within France'). Their endurance was about three hours (as they were over water for 'exactly two hours'), but their altitude was probably modest, with descent a greater concern. The pilot had to jettison 'coat and trowsers' as well as operate a 'curious expedient' which many a cold, frightened or long-standing aeronaut has chosen to let loose, whether or not short of altitude.

Jean Pierre Blanchard not only received 100,000 livres and a life pension for his piloting endeavour (as against his accompanying sponsor who earned zilch) but acquired a steady zest for further pioneering. He was first to fly in Germany, Holland, Belgium, Switzerland, Poland, and the Czech republic as well as the United States (all within eight years). His greatest distance flown, achieved seven months after the Channel, was 300 miles. And his greatest altitude, wholly unbelievable, was 32,000 feet (in 1798). He did not become the first aviation casualty, as Jean-François Pilâtre de Rozier and Jules Romain had earlier acquired that distinction when attempting to cross the

Channel from France to England, but was unhappily first to experience heart attack when airborne (and to die from its effects one year later). Without doubt, during his 60 flights, he became number one achiever in the aeronautic pantheon. (And 10 years later, albeit posthumously, he scored another first – of

Oddest, most bizarre, most impractical, most (seemingly) practical – humans have to compete, to exhibit prowess, to do better (or worse) than the next in line.

sorts – when an aviation accident also killed his wife.)

Who is pantheon's number two is less clear, there being a quantity of deserving pioneers during the following years. James Sadler, first English aeronaut, certainly merits mention, having once reportedly achieved 112 miles in 80 minutes. Later he failed to cross from Ireland to England, but in that attempt did travel 43 miles over the Irish countryside and 237 over water before 'landing' in the sea where a sailor cleverly speared the foundering balloon with the boat's bowsprit, thereby rescuing both balloon and undamaged aeronaut. Sadler's son Windham succeeded in crossing that Irish Sea in 1817, travelling from Dublin to Anglesey in five and a half hours. Unfortunately the courageous Windham died seven years later, after being 'dashed' against a chimney in high wind before 'plunging' to the ground, whereas his father, premier English balloonist, died in his bed in 1828, having made 50 ascents during his lifetime.

During the first century of ballooning it was not necessarily easy to break records, but there were so many waiting to be broken. Tétu-Brissy, Frenchman, was first to fly at night (remaining airborne for 11 hours in 1786) and first to ascend on horseback (in 1798), a style of feat popular in early days for which enthusiasm then waned. Francisque Arban, another Frenchman, was first to cross the European Alps, travelling safely from Marseilles to Turin (but dying in the Mediterranean one month later on a flight from Barcelona). Rufus Wells, American, helped to establish the sport of multi-country travelling (not unknown today) by flying in South America, Australia, Europe (in general), Egypt, Java, India and Japan. 'If this is Java it must be...'. André Garnerin, Frenchman, was first to descend by parachute (in 1797). His wife then became first woman to do so, and his niece Elisa – not to be outdone – became the first professional woman parachutist, giving 39 parachute displays between 1815 and 1836.

It is tempting to linger with such early heroes, but the major milestones of distance, height and endurance deserve sharper focus. The first determined distance attempt occurred in November 1836. Charles Green (pilot), Thomas Mason (flautist, patron of the arts, sponsor) and Robert Hollond (M.P. for

The first 'Breitling Orbiter' got as far as the Mediterranean from Switzerland. The second, one year later, broke records by reaching Myanmar.

Hastings) decided to travel further than anyone had ever done. To assist them they took 186 lb of provisions (another early record) and 1,000 feet of trail-rope. This would glide over the land beneath, thus stabilising their height but casually destabilising, one presumes, much ground-based furnishing. Their ballast, equipment and provisions, with two gallons of brandy, two of sherry and two of port swelling the consumables, totalled 2,763 lb (which must have been another first).

Take-off was from Vauxhall Gardens, London, into a wind from the north-west. The balloonists missed Canterbury

cathedral by two miles, which was fortunate for Canterbury cathedral, and they also missed Calais after it had loomed abruptly from the dark. Their speed was 25 miles an hour and all Europe then lay before them. They were much impressed by the glow from belching iron-works, and then by the colours of dawn. Believing they might have reached 'Poland or Russia' (another first in miscalculation) they landed at 7.30 am to discover they were near Weilburg, some 30 miles north-west of Frankfurt-am-Main, Germany. Although well to the west of their assumed location they had achieved the world's longest flight, having travelled 480 miles during the 18 hours since take-off.

Altitude was not their concern. Once the earliest balloonists had proved that respiration was still possible above ground level there was little initial interest in going higher than was necessary. Mountaineers were saying that temperature fell by 1°F. for every 300 feet of ascent, but there was no immediate enthusiasm for balloons and their balloonists to clinch the matter. In any case an aeronaut's claimed altitude generally led to dissent. The first high flight, with science as its spur, was promoted by the French Academy of Sciences in 1803 and piloted by Etienne Robertson. He claimed not only an altitude of 23,526 feet but the discovery that human heads swell with increasing height, his hat allegedly becoming less than serviceable (and his whole story then less than immediately believable).

One year later, again promoted by the Academy (which may have had second thoughts about Robertson), Nicolas François Gay-Lussac took to the air, reaching/claiming 22,892 feet. His barometer also asserted, most competitively, that Robertson and his similar instrument could only have reached 21,400 feet. There were various subsequent claims (and counter-claims) concerning altitude, for example by Charles Green of England, Jungins of Germany, Barral and Bixio of France, and John Welsh of London, Kew Observatory, but there was always doubt and disagreement until James Glaisher entered the lists. This Fellow of the Royal Society was not only of a different style and calibre, but worked at a later date when science in all its forms had advanced most distinctively.

The year of 1862 was his pinnacle and Henry Coxwell his pilot. All three of their flights started from Wolverhampton, suitably central for high altitude endeavour. The first reached

The Atlantic Ocean killed five before being conquered by balloon. To humiliate it further, Don Cameron arranged a race of five balloons across it in 1992. He (at left) and Rob Bayly flew from Maine to Portugal.

26,000 feet and ended in Rutland, that touch-down smashing much of their scientific equipment. The second achieved 24,000 feet, landing more gently near Solihull. The third, and quite the most remarkable, started on 5 September at 1 pm (having been delayed by bad weather – so what else is new?). At 11,000 feet they broke through cloud to be rewarded by brilliant, blinding and gorgeous sunshine. One hour and 50 minutes after take-off they reached 26,400 feet, genuinely higher than every earlier achievement.

Their balloon was then still rising, having gained 5,000 feet in the previous 10 minutes, and Glaisher was first to feel the effects of such extreme (and sudden) altitude. He saw that the barometer's mercury stood at 9.75 inches, indicating 29,000 feet, but then he lost the use of both his arms. Soon he slumped down, observing Coxwell above him, but he could no longer speak. Darkness then 'overcame' him, his eyes having become 'insensible'. Coxwell was also in trouble, as his hands had 'gone black', but at 2 hours 4 minutes after take-off (when the balloon had presumably descended to a slightly lower altitude) both men started to recover. Scientific observation began again at 2 hours 7 minutes, the period of unconsciousness for Glaisher having lasted several minutes. Their terrifying flight ended at 2 hours 50 minutes in Shropshire, less than 23 miles from their starting point. Neither man (aged 43 and 53) suffered from the experience, with Glaisher (senior of the two) promptly walking seven miles to Ludlow for balloon conveyance (and not dying until reaching the age of 94).

Far less certain is the height they actually achieved when both men were in trouble. Glaisher, although aware of his unconsciousness, asserted that 37,000 feet had been their maximum. In which case it is astonishing they did not die. They must also have descended very rapidly, dropping seven miles in 45 minutes, a not impossible feat but hasty none-the-less. Without wishing to denigrate an undoubted hero it is probable that 30,000 feet is nearer the mark – or slightly higher than Mount Everest.

The next high altitude ascent, made by three Frenchmen 13 years later, was much less fortunate. Glaisher had flown without oxygen, but the three from Paris took bladders containing an air-oxygen mix. At 22,800 feet they revived themselves with this stimulant and, feeling better, jettisoned ballast. The pilot, Gaston Tissandier, then lost consciousness but recovered his wits soon afterwards when the balloon was rapidly descending. He

therefore discarded ballast, but one of the others wrongfully assisted him by tossing overboard a further 80 lb of scientific instrument. All three men then lost their sensibility as the balloon climbed once more.

When Tissandier recovered for the second time his balloon was, yet again, descending rapidly, but his two scientific companions, with blood congealed from mouths and noses, were plainly dead. This disturbing discovery did not prevent him making a satisfactory landing, an atterrissage much favoured as subject matter by publishers of the day. The subsequent publicity presumably discouraged others from further attempts at altitude until Berson of Germany picked up the gauntlet, reaching 30,000 feet in 1894. Seven years later (in 1901) he and a companion achieved 35,500 feet, also losing consciousness for part of the time (as had become traditional). Auguste Piccard of Switzerland then took control of altitude by using a pressurised container. He ballooned up to 53,153 feet in 1932.

The invention of the aeroplane undoubtedly put paid to much pioneering enterprise concerning balloons. Aircraft were going faster, higher, further, seemingly with every year that passed. Airships were also doing amazing things, not so much with altitude but in distance and endurance, dropping a cross at the North Pole, casually cruising from Europe both to Rio and New York on a regular basis, and even circumnavigating the globe (with the Graf Zeppelin) in four triumphant hops. What price balloons, therefore, when all these powered triumphs were being so remarkable?

The major exception to this general dismissal lay in the Gordon Bennett races. James Gordon Bennett, owner of the New York Herald (and financier of Henry Stanley's mission to find David Livingstone 35 years earlier), was 65 when he gave a cup to the Fédération Aéronautique Internationale. It was to be awarded on behalf of the balloonist who flew furthest from a specified location. The rules were simple. No nation could enter more than three balloons. All inflations had to be with the same kind of gas. Order of take-off would be decided by ballot. And the distance flown thereafter was all that mattered.

There had been nothing like it before (save for the automobile, 'motor-flying' and airship races inspired earlier by the same Gordon Bennett, none of which had created such popular interest as his final sponsorship). The first balloon race started on 30 September 1906, from the Tuileries Gardens in Paris (in honour and commemoration of Jacques Charles's pioneering ascent from the same spot 123 years earlier). Sixteen balloons took off into a south-easterly wind. Nine of them stopped short of the English Channel, and of the remaining

Richard Branson (left) and Per Lindstrand, with the Atlantic and Pacific Oceans beneath their belts, inevitably cast their eyes upon a circumnavigation of the world.

seven Frank Lahm travelled furthest (404 miles) by landing at Fylingdales in Yorkshire, not far south of Whitby. The race of 1907 was therefore held in the United States, that being the winner's nation.

The greatest distance flown in the 26 races held between 1906 and 1938 was 1,369 miles when Bienaimé, a Frenchman, flew from Stuttgart, Germany, to land near St Petersburg, Russia, after 45 hours and 42 minutes. The longest time spent aloft followed the ascent of two Swiss individuals from Berlin in 1908. They landed near Kristiansund in Norway after 73 hours and 1 minute. Most of those hours had been spent over the North Sea which they had first encountered after over-flying Kiel. They then flew north as far as the Arctic Circle, and were en route for Spitzbergen when a relenting wind reversed direction, bringing them south to the location of their Norwegian touchdown. Their straight-line distance from start to finish was a mere 808 miles, but calculations showed they had actually flown 932 miles further, thus making an unofficial total of 1,740 miles.

Controversy began when it was learned that a ship had towed the Swiss balloon into port. Despite being told (in several languages) 'not to touch the trail-rope' a ship's captain had

persisted in doing so – hence immediate calls from several balloon crews for Swiss disqualification. 'Unlawful assistance had been given and should be penalised'. The general council of the FAI was called upon to adjudicate. It experienced considerable debate before 39 delegates voted in favour of the Swiss team, with 13 against and six abstentions. Switzerland was therefore permitted to win the famous cup, a feat it only accomplished once more (in 1921).

Until World War Two called a halt to this most international and peaceful pastime only six nations of the 14 which had competed ever won the race. They were Belgium (seven times), France (once), Germany (twice), Poland (four times), Switzerland (twice) and the United States (10 times). Great Britain flew on 13 of the 26 occasions and managed to be second twice (in 1906 and 1921). On the single occasion when Charles Rolls flew (1906) this aviation and automobile enthusiast achieved a creditable third place, travelling from Paris to the vicinity of the Wash in eastern England, a flight of 288 miles which lasted for 26 hours and 18 minutes.

The 27th Gordon Bennett race was scheduled to start from Lwow (then in Poland) on 3 September 1939, Poland (and Antoni Janusz) having won the event in 1938 by flying 1,057 miles in 37 hours and 47 minutes from Liège, Belgium, to Riga in Latvia. With terrible irony that same week had also been selected by Germany for its invasion of Poland, this event sparking off World War Two. A most laudable sport, with competing nations happily crossing each other's frontiers, therefore became its horrific counterpart with warring nationalities being brutally casual of those same borders.

When peace had been regained, and with traditional activities to the fore once more, there was no mention of long-distance flying until, quite suddenly, 1958. The Small World, a gas balloon of 60,000 cubic feet, had been constructed (by the RFD company), and a most improbable foursome were to be its crew. Arnold Eiloart, without earlier experience of ballooning, did try learning, and did fly, but he resented the strictures of instruction and his instructors responded by resenting him. The eventual debacle of a take-off from the Canary Islands did lead – just – to flight, but left little expectation that the courageous foursome might reach the Atlantic's other side, as they intended. In the end their craft travelled 1,450 miles before dropping to the sea. The gas-filled envelope was then released and their gondola became, as skilfully conceived, an effective and serviceable boat.

Most aeronauts will do almost anything to avoid water, but The Small World's crew were mariners more than aviators. The Mudie pair, Colin and Rosemary, are famous for designing many kinds of boat (such as replicas of vessels from the past) and the Eiloart couple, father and son, were also more familiar with water than the air. The world in general was both mystified and alarmed by their weeks-long disappearance after take-off, but friends and colleagues who knew them best were not surprised when the foursome sailed into Barbados, a touch thinner and very weary, but happily safe and sound. Their boat of a gondola plus their nautical experience had jointly served them well.

The Small World's distance flown was short of the world gas balloon record – two Russians had flown 1,987.6 miles in 1950 – but it undoubtedly focussed attention upon the Atlantic. To cross that formidable hurdle and acquire the blue riband for distance suddenly held a double appeal. There had been 19th century endeavour in this direction, coupled with experimental trials over land, but no real assault upon the ocean had taken place, save for The Small World's extraordinary feat (which was all the more remarkable for attempting to cross from east to west).

Charles Green, hero of the London-Frankfurt flight, had spoken of the idea. So too John Wise, a later and American balloonist, who even suspended a lifeboat beneath his envelope, but was forced to discard it during a trial flight before also jettisoning the idea. Thaddeus Lowe, later famous for balloon observation in the Civil War, constructed a trans-Atlantic hopeful of 725,000 cubic feet, only to see it destroyed by a squall in 1859. The Daily Graphic balloon, built in 1873 with the same intent, crashed into the Catskill mountains, this mishap cancelling the project in similar style. Long-distance flying then lapsed, and all such thoughts were further eclipsed when powered aviation occupied the skies.

Then came the 1960s, with world wars in the past, with aircraft flying the world's oceans in routine style, with a happy hippy attitude to life and, most significantly for long-distance ballooning endeavour, with thoughts of crossing the Atlantic adamantly whetted by The Small World's brave attempt. Two Canadians took off in 1968, only to ditch not far from Nova Scotia shortly afterwards. Two years later a couple of Americans ascended from Long Island in a more determined venture, with Malcolm Brighton of Britain (my old Wasp accomplice) as their pilot. They too were forced to ditch, well to the south-east of Newfoundland, and may even have beaten the existing distance record before all three vanished to leave no trace either of themselves or their Free Life balloon.

Then came the Yankee Zephyr which ascended from Maine in 1973. Its solo pilot was rescued when in trouble also near Newfoundland. Light Heart took off one year later from Pennsylvania with a single pilot, but neither Thomas Gatch nor his balloon was ever found. The Spirit of Man departed from New Jersey in 1974, but the balloon exploded shortly afterwards, killing Bob Berger, its single occupant. In short, and thus far, the beguiling Atlantic had inspired five 20th century attempts and had also claimed five lives.

Ed Yost, the stoical and resolute pioneer of propane flying, then felt compelled to step into this ring. Three more American balloons, Windborne, Odyssey and Spirit of '76 had all tried and failed before he ascended from Maine in October 1976 in Silver Fox, a gas balloon. After flying for 107 hours and 37 minutes, and having encountered a northerly wind, he was forced to descend 200 miles from the Azores, having travelled for a great-circle (and record) distance of 2,475 miles. The actual crossing had eluded him, but this too was achieved only two years later when three other Americans (in a Yost-built balloon with a Mudie-style gondola) also ascended from Maine. In Double Eagle II they not only traversed the Atlantic but continued over England to land in France less than 60 miles from Paris after 137 hours and 5 minutes. Their officially calculated distance was 3,120 miles. This single flight therefore most emphatically broke both the endurance and distance records of the time, as well as humbling the Atlantic Ocean.

It was to be humbled even more in the years to come. In 1984 Joe Kittinger, already renowned for parachuting from 102,000 feet, ballooned single-handedly over the Atlantic to touch down in Italy – a great circle distance of 3,544.3 miles. (His parachuting flight beneath a balloon did not count as a balloon altitude record because balloons must land with the same personnel on board as at the start.) Two years later a couple of Dutchmen not only crossed but landed, as they had hoped (and planned), in Holland. In 1987 Per Lindstrand and Richard Branson flew across in a hot-air balloon, thereby achieving a world distance record for such balloons by travelling for 2,787.9 miles. In 1992 two Spaniards were first to cross from East to West, starting from the Canary Islands (as with The Small World) and landing in Venezuela. They travelled 3,200 miles in five and half days beneath a 60,000 cubic foot Rozière balloon, the combination type exploiting the advantages both of gas and of hot air.

In that same year, as greatest humiliation of them all, a balloon race was organised over the ocean which, only 14 years beforehand, had never even been crossed. Don Cameron, founder of Bristol-based Cameron Balloons, was its promoter. He had attempted the Atlantic (with Chris Davey) 16 days before the first successful (and American) crossing, but had been forced to meet the sea when 108 miles short of France. His revenge – if that is the word – was to arrange for five balloons to compete across the hurdle which had led to his earlier defeat. They were all Rozières and, at 77,000 cubic feet each, a touch larger than the Spanish version (also built by Camerons). The five trans-Atlantic competitors, each with a two-man crew, took off at short intervals on 16 September 1992 from Bangor, Maine.

One of the crews was forced to ditch after 82 hours, another after 121 hours (when only 30 miles from land) and both these teams were speedily rescued. Don himself, with his co-pilot Rob Bayly, travelled 3,014 miles during 124 hours and 6 minutes before touching down on a Portuguese beach. The race was won, in that their balloon landed first on the Atlantic's eastern side, by Wim Verstraeten (of Belgium) and Bertrand Piccard (of Switzerland). They touched down in Spain, having travelled for 3,081 miles in only 119 hours and 20 minutes. The actual distance and endurance winners, crushing all earlier such records, were Troy Bradley and Richard Abruzzo, both from the United States. They eventually reached Morocco, having taken 144 hours and 52 minutes to travel 3,332 miles. The whole race was therefore a formidable achievement, with drama, rescue, comradeship, rivalry and broken records all happily intertwined. As for the Atlantic it had been transformed from an insuperable (and all too lethal) obstacle into a convenient stretch of water over which aspiring balloonists could test their skill.

Individuals who wish to become a world leader in ballooning can choose one of numerous categories. Not only are free-flying balloons classified into five 'sub-classes' but there are 15 categories of size. The sub-classes are:

AA The standard form of gas balloon.
AX Standard hot air balloons.
AM (also known as Rozières) Combination balloons, with heaters warming gas.
AS Balloons using pressurised gas.
AT Any balloon not falling into any of those four other categories.

The smallest of the 15 sizes involves all balloons up to 250 cubic metres in volume (8,828 cubic feet). The largest includes all balloons greater than 22,000 cubic metres (776,836 cubic feet). It would therefore be possible, in theory, for a single and most ardently competitive balloonist to be world champion 75

The author, two feet off the ground.

times over, making use of all the categories and all the sizes.

His wife could also do the same, as there is a similar range of possibilities strictly for females. As women are not debarred from holding the world records (which are open to all) it was inevitably argued that no need existed for separate female achievements. The counter-argument stated that this gender distinction gave pleasure – to some, and no noticeable displeasure to anyone. Therefore world records (as of now) are available to all, and the separate female records are only for

Make 'em bigger. Give 'em double-decker baskets. Make 'em go faster, further, higher. Biggest (in 1974) was the Heineken balloon.

females (with either the solitary pilot or the entire airborne crew being of that sex).

The three prime records of interest to balloonists concern the greatest achievements – ever – for distance, duration and altitude. Currently the distance record stands at 10,360.61 miles (16,673.33 km) flown by J. Stephen Fossett when he travelled in January 1997 from St Louis, Missouri, to northern India. With the same flight he also won the duration time by staying aloft for 6 days, 2 hours and 44 minutes. As for altitude that was won by Cdr M. D. Ross and Lt/Cdr V. A. Prather in May 1961 when they ascended to 34,668 metres (113,711 feet), having taken off from USS Antietam in the Gulf of Mexico. These three pinnacles,

all won by Americans, are the Absolute World Records for free-flying man-carrying balloons, irrespective of size, of numbers on board or any other variable.

Stephen Fossett, winner of two-thirds of these prime accolades (who had never been in a balloon until 1993), has numerous other achievements on which he can reflect. Firstly (and, perhaps, most critically of all) he has made a heap of money, and is still in business (but not full time) as a 'stock-options investor'. He can therefore finance his various obsessions, all of which seem as single-mindedly competitive as the cut-and-thrust of Chicago's money market. He has climbed the highest mountains on several continents, save for Everest (despite trying twice). He has swum the English Channel – at his fourth attempt. Crossing the Dardanelles was easier, in that he swum it both ways. He has world records in single-handed sailing – across the Pacific, for example. He has driven dogsleds in Alaska (in the Iditarod race), competed in triathlons, and looks about as athletic as, well, a stock-options investor. He lives high in the Colorado mountains and is married, but without children to help him spend his wealth. He was 52 when flying from Missouri all the way to India.

Having ballooned solo across the Pacific (from Seoul in South Korea to Leader in Saskatchewan, a distance of 5,467 miles) it was inevitable, remembering his track record in other events when he had attempted to better his best, that thoughts of a circumnavigation would cross his mind. In fact, no sooner did they cross than he put them into action. And no sooner initiated than, or so it seemed, he was ascending from South Dakota with the whole world spread ahead of him. Unfortunately there were difficulties with the envelope, and there were also problems with firing the motor to charge his batteries (for radio transmissions). After only two days he landed – 'it's all most embarrassing,' said the pilot – in New Brunswick, Canada, having not even left North America. People who try Everest again, and the English Channel again (and again) do not withdraw merely because a few obstacles have arisen. They buy another (bigger and better) envelope, and wait for the following year.

Stephen Fossett's extraordinary achievement in 1997, when he broke those two absolute world records, was all the more remarkable for succeeding so brilliantly when his two other circum-global rivals had failed so absolutely. Moreover his balloon was cheaper than either of theirs, and much simpler. Theirs had pressurised capsules; his did not. Theirs had crews to fly them, with teams of three men and two men respectively; he was on his own. They had intended to fly high within the jet-streams; he would have to be at a lower level, owing to his open gondola. Their balloons had been heavily sponsored; he had received no financial support from any company. Prior to the flight, and as an individual, Stephen Fossett had been unobtrusive, refraining from press conferences and being generally inconspicuous. (So much so that Richard Branson, having flown to watch his rival's ascent, was chatting to an onlooker within the St Louis stadium when, with cameras suddenly looming, he abruptly realised his casual acquaintance was none other than the man in charge.)

Fossett's cheaper, simpler and more relaxed endeavour did gain by starting after the two earlier ventures. Richard Branson and his team had selected Marrakech, Morocco, for their launch site, this place having modest surface winds and being nearer to the all-important jet-streams. They had first travelled there in the winter of 1995/6, together with the Global Challenger balloon, but that season had finished without the upper winds and surface conditions being suitable simultaneously. When the winter of 1996/7 arrived it was reassembly time for Branson, Per Lindstrand (pilot and manufacturer) and Rory McCarthy (businessman and adventurer). They reached Marrakech in January 1997, together with their ground crew and a considerable force of merry journalists.

Lower and upper winds both obliged on 7 January. The Branson balloon took off, with him and Per on board plus engineer Alex Ritchie, last minute replacement for Rory (a temporary chest infection having forbidden his inclusion). From the start nothing went well. Some couplings had been left attached (causing Alex to engage, most courageously, in what astronauts call extra-vehicular activity) and the rapid ascent helped to precipitate a rapid descent. On board they realised that circumnavigation was out of the question, and therefore chose to land within the emptiness of neighbouring Algeria, safe and sound but having travelled for only 20 hours and 400 miles.

Four days later the second competitor took off from Chateau d'Oex, Switzerland. Financed by Breitling, and built by Cameron (as with Fossett's balloon), Don Cameron himself launched this further challenger. On board were Bertrand Piccard (of Switzerland and of the famous record-breaking family for going either up or down) and Wim Verstraeten (of Belgium, also with an Atlantic balloon crossing beneath his belt). Take-off was perfect, but a leaking kerosene pipe within the capsule put paid to that attempt on the same day as the launch. The Breitling team had chosen this fuel for heating (unlike Fossett and Lindstrand who preferred propane). One small connector then failed, thereby venting noxious and – in sufficient concentration – lethal fumes. Bertrand and Wim elected for a Mediterranean ditching when still close to the rescue services of southern France.

Two days later the unassuming Fossett stood with his Solo Spirit balloon inside the Busch Stadium at St Louis, Missouri (not only his wife's home town but famous as generous supporter, via several philanthropists, of Charles Lindbergh's solo Atlantic crossing 70 years earlier). The two earlier and costly balloon attempts had failed. Their very experienced teams had failed. These others had been the favourites, as judged by journalists, and had each succumbed. It is difficult to call a millionaire like Fossett an under-dog, particularly when he has extracted $300,000 from his own pocket to pay for the venture, but that was the general feeling within the stadium. And that, in part, was why the cheering was quite so loud when he triumphed so tremendously in journeying beneath a free-flying balloon from Missouri in the United States to Uttar Pradesh in India.

On board his capsule he had considerable communications equipment, partly for contacting his ground team in Chicago. Having informed them that his landing was due, a decision to end the flight having been precipitated by thunder-clouds in the general area (and by considerable tiredness after six demanding days), Fossett confirmed he would be in touch when safely down on earth. Chicago then waited, and continued to wait, becoming increasingly anxious after an hour had become two and then three.

Meanwhile the adventuring millionaire, his equipment quite unharmed, and he too equally unscathed, was informing the gathering Indians of his need to call Chicago. At once, most helpfully, they took him to the nearest village (proving to be not so near) which had a public phone. When he arrived there was a queue. He was also short of change and it took a while, quite a long while, before Chicago could leap up and down after hearing confirmation that their man was safe, sound, and still with a few wits about him, if not all, so starved was he of sleep. Or perhaps all his wits were solidly in place. 'Friends' affirm that he saved money by using a conventional land-line rather than his hi-tech devices which, more expensively, exploited satellites.

The 'global season' of 1997/8, despite lessons learned from the earlier northern winter, did not start off too well. Richard Branson, Per Lindstrand and Alex Ritchie were all set to fly from

Marrakech in early January when their balloon's envelope escaped during the procedure of inflation (and did not return to earth again until reaching Algeria). The inflation team blamed a sudden gust – and also the decision to inflate during the daytime when such gusts are more probable.

Steve Fossett then ascended from the same Missouri stadium he had used in 1997. All went well initially, with the United States and the Atlantic soon left behind, but extremely unsettled weather then hindered his chances (and he flew over Britain during an extremely vicious and turbulent weekend). On reaching eastern Europe it became plain that his earlier records would elude him. The weather was not being co-operative, his heating system was failing, one burner was proving troublesome, and he was being forced to admit defeat, both in failing to encompass the globe and doing less well than on his previous attempt. A trouble-free landing was achieved on a huge field near Krasnodar, southern Russia, with the authorities in this area determinedly helpful.

In quick succession there then came three mishaps. Kevin Uliassi ascended solo from a sheltered quarry near Chicago. Two hours later he heard a terrific bang, and quickly realised the helium cell of his balloon had ruptured. There was no point in continuing his global endeavour, and he carefully flew his balloon down to effect a satisfactory landing. Dick Rutan and Dave Melton then took off from Albuquerque, New Mexico, and also experienced a rupture of their helium cell shortly afterwards. With both balloons manufactured in similar fashion by Cameron Balloons it was speculated that some fundamental fault must be involved. Or that the ascent had been too rapid. Or that inexperience (with the ways of Roziere balloons) had contributed to the downfall of both these aerostats. Rutan and Melton elected to abandon their crippled craft, and separately parachuted from its gondola. Melton was injured by his landing, and Rutan had painful cause to regret the prevalence of cacti in desert environments. Meanwhile, the balloon, relieved of its crew, floated eastwards, occasionally hitting the ground and finally coming to rest near Gainesville, Texas, some 45 miles north of Dallas.

The third (and graver) mishap concerned Alex Ritchie, Branson's flight engineer who had achieved renown during the

Houses and olive trees in Morocco, just downwind from Marrakech where the Branson balloon took off with high hopes – only to land a short while later in Algeria. Balloons might have been flying for 215 years, but they still captivate, whenever, wherever, however.

Steve Fossett, after his third attempt to balloon around the world, having come to earth in southern Russia.

earlier Branson flight by climbing from the capsule's security to release some couplings which, had they remained intact, would have seriously imperilled the lives of all three crewmen. For the 1998 venture, and while waiting at Marrakech, he accepted an opportunity to improve his parachuting skills. Unfortunately, as his canopy opened, he suffered injury. On hitting the ground, already doubled up in pain, he received far more injury, with every limb broken and, yet more troubling, many organs damaged. He was flown swiftly to London's Middlesex Hospital, and he died three months later, having been in intensive care for most of that time.

The Breitling balloon, successor to the 1997 version which had been ditched in the Mediterranean after flying from Switzerland, was being actively prepared while these other misadventures were occurring. On board, as before, would be Bertrand Piccard and Wim Verstraeten, but with the addition of Andy Elson as 'flight engineer'. This particular Briton, adventurer

by nature, ardent parachutist and trans-Everest balloonist, proved to be a vital member of the crew.

At first, even before take-off from Chateau d'Oex in Switzerland, things did not go smoothly. The capsule, with all its kerosene on board, was being lifted by crane into position when a crucial fastening snapped. The subsequent drop was, most fortunately, only a few inches, but damage did occur. A couple of weeks later, with repairs effected and the weather good, a satisfactory ascent was achieved, this event almost immediately followed by news that the capsule was not airtight. Andy, the new recruit (seemingly happiest when nothing but air exists between him and the ground), had to climb out of the gondola, remove some suspect grit from the sealing of a lower hatch cover, and then scramble back in again.

Fortunately the seal was then secure, and the balloon could safely ascend to a decent altitude where jet-streams would be found. Unfortunately – with bad news tending to follow good in every form of pioneering – the departure from Switzerland meant, initially at least, flying well to the north of such speedy air currents. Going high was pointless if speed over the ground was not improved. Therefore, for an agonising couple of days, the Breitling trio had good views of the Mediterranean as they loitered southwards, forever hoping it would soon be opportune to enter the fast lane up above. They flew over the Strait of Bonifacio, lying between Corsica and Sardinia, and then headed east for Italy. Suddenly there was talk of Israel or Syria, with the flight entering quite another phase.

Those of us with feet currently anchored to the ground could, no less suddenly, feel envy for the three on board as we began to visualise the flight lying ahead of Breitling's capsule. Just think of the trip which they eventually enjoyed! To begin with they travelled almost the entire length of the Mediterranean, not a bad journey in itself. Then came the Syrian desert before crossing the Euphrates and the Tigris. Straight over Baghdad, and next across the Zagros mountains to the flat central plateau of Iran (with both Iraq and Iran, politically at odds with much of the world, 'exceedingly co-operative'). Soon came Afghanistan and Pakistan, and then low (and slow) over India – even within sight of the Taj Mahal – while permission to enter Chinese airspace was being formally requested (and, at first, formally refused). Lower travel also meant conversation with those down below, and children running in company as children are so wont to do.

China did then yield permission, but the leisurely flying – initially and then latterly, plus a mysterious fuel leakage at the outset – meant that the tremendous hurdle of the Pacific was too much to contemplate. Therefore where to end the flight? After leaving India, and on encountering the Bay of Bengal, it was decided that Myanmar (the old Burma) would be satisfactory. During the ninth day after leaving Switzerland, and when approaching Rangoon/Yangon, the Breitling balloon was coerced to land, eventually doing so in a rice paddy 75 miles from the capital with no trouble at all.

Amazingly, and forewarned of the probable destination, the ground crew from Bristol were (almost) in attendance, having flown in a private jet from Switzerland. Yet more amazingly Phil Dunnington, of Cameron Balloons (makers of the *Breitling Orbiter*), was already in Myanmar, and at Mandalay, negotiating a balloon sale. He dropped everything, hired a helicopter, and was at the launch site as the balloon came to rest in a one-knot wind for a stand-up landing. The Road to Mandalay, where – so said Kipling – flying fishes play, was abruptly host to a flying fish (of sorts) which had broken all records for airborne endurance.

Its on-board threesome had voyaged for 9 days, 17 hours and 55 minutes. They had beaten Steve Fossett's record by 3 days, 15 hours and 5 minutes (and Fossett had nobly congratulated them, via their Swiss control centre, the moment they eclipsed the endurance record he had achieved slightly over one year earlier). From Switzerland and the River Rhone to Myanmar and the Irrawaddy is an extraordinary voyage even in these days of long-distance travel. To achieve it by free-flying balloon, with only the exuberance of the wind as transport agent, is a whole dimension more remarkable.

The single certainty is that this achievement will not stay long with its pre-eminence. Envy among others, on hearing of the flight, will be transformed into rivalry. The winter of 1998/9 will assuredly be witness to further competition, each entrant hoping to go further than Fossett, or stay up longer than the Breitling men, or merely to savour a little of the joy and astonishment which these predecessors have already experienced. Attempts to circumnavigate the globe will not diminish because others have failed – on the contrary. The lapses will whet appetite; just you wait and see!

CHAPTER **15**

What next?

No one anticipated the extraordinary rise in ballooning which has taken place in the past 40 years. No one can possibly forecast what can/will happen in the next 40 years.
Surely the future rise cannot be so great. Or can it?
And what might happen in years to come?

WHAT INDEED! Niels Bohr, brilliant nuclear physicist, once said: 'Prediction is very difficult, especially about the future.' At no time during the past four decades, and since those of us who are longer in the tooth first saw a free balloon, could we have predicted – with any expectation of accuracy – today's situation. Similarly, when Raven Industries was making the first hot-air flight over the English Channel, it could not have been possible for the two on board to have imagined that 60+ balloons now cross that same stretch of water on occasion, a massive and enchanting invasion of the European continent (much like many early prints depicting military might via lighter-than-air).

Could anyone have foreseen, during early meets when 10 balloons were most impressively gathered in one place, that the population increase of aerostats would be quite so dramatic? Balloons and Airships of the World 1997 (compiled by Mel Kirby) lists 17,000 balloon registrations from over 60 manufacturers. There is no indication that balloon creation is about to halt, with Britain now host to four manufacturers, a number bigger than ever in the past. They are Sky Balloons (the newest), Lindstrand Balloons (so linked with Richard Branson spectaculars), Cameron Balloons (oldest and biggest), and Thunder & Colt (purchased by Camerons, but maintaining independence).

Could Don Cameron himself have guessed, when he turned one room of his Cotham Park home in Bristol into a ballooning factory (of sorts), that he would first expand into a decommissioned church and then, that also becoming too small, into a tremendous former warehouse, suitable site for 130 employees? Could he even have guessed more recently, after purchasing Thunder & Colt as a going concern following its failure to survive, that it would independently land the biggest single balloon order there has ever been, namely 11 balloons for the Michelin centenary, some special-shaped – as Michelin Men – and others of more conventional design?

More balloons now fly in the United States than in any other nation, as any forecaster could have predicted (knowing of its wealth), but could that same prophet also have imagined that balloon proliferation would reach so great a multitude of other nations, big, small, rich, poor, and likely or improbable recipients of this latest (as well as earliest) craze of aviation? British balloons have been sold to expected destinations, such as Canada, France, Italy, Sweden, Switzerland and Japan, but also to Bahrain, Belarus, Myanmar, Iran, Monaco, Bulgaria, Macedonia, Slovenia, Lebanon, Poland, Nepal, Libya, Latvia, Namibia, Ukraine, China, Estonia, Albania and Zimbabwe, for example. In all, and thus far, a total of 73 countries have bought a balloon from Britain. Who, in 1970, or 1980, or even 1990 could have foreseen such an export industry?

As for the breaking of further barriers, of achieving what has not yet been achieved, it is difficult – at first – to think of further obstacles to be overcome. The Atlantic and the Pacific have been conquered. The long-distance record for free-flying balloons stands at over 10,000 miles. Endurance is over six days. As for height there is the plan (by Colin Prescot and Per Lindstrand) to beat the existing record by 15,000 feet. Ross and Prather ascended to 113,740 feet in 1961, and the Prescot/Lindstrand target is 130,000 feet. Atmospheric pressure at that altitude is less than 1 per cent of the sea-level quantity. In consequence the balloon will be 275 times larger in volume at that height than when standing on the ground. Its two high-flyers will regard the curvature of the earth not from a capsule but from space-suits. Should these suits be damaged the two men will perish instantly.

The breaking of further barriers will continue, partly because a balloon is not so much an entity as exploitation of a principle. As from 1783 balloons have used the fundamental fact that a bag of something lighter than the surrounding medium will create lift. That lift, generated first by hot smoke and (no doubt) impure hydrogen, enabled four courageous individuals to fly in aviation's first momentous year. It will also send (if all goes well) Colin and Per 24 miles above the ground. It sent Fossett almost half way round the earth. It sends all lesser mortals into the air when, with our smaller aerostats, we fly, smoothly or erratically, high or low, fast or slow, above nearby countryside. As for the future there will surely be other reasons for generating lift by the same old principle, and the things exploiting it will – no doubt – be called balloons.

Human beings are not going to give up their passion for pushing frontiers back, for going one step further, for doing slightly better than someone else. Conventional ballooning will continue to go higher, further, faster, longer, with fewer people than ever before or more people than ever before. What about twice around the world? Or 30 miles high? Or 100 in a basket at one time? There are no limits and, even if there were, humans would try to prove that there were not.

The number of 'last great adventures' which have been staged in recent decades has been phenomenal, whether crossing Antarctica from coast to coast, crossing it without assistance, crossing it solo, climbing Everest, climbing it as a major group, climbing it the hard way, climbing without oxygen, reaching the very bottom of the deepest ocean, flying around the world without refuelling, sailing single-handedly around the world, sailing without stopping, sailing the 'wrong' way round also without stopping. At this very moment there are, most assuredly, further 'last great adventures' being planned, and there will be lots more last adventures when the current final efforts have reached the record books.

So too with ballooning. Having watched this sport grow and grow ever since I first became involved I have been amazed, over and over again, by its progress. When I flew by gas balloon over the Straits of Zanzibar to land on Africa that endeavour made front page news. By today's standards it was a puny adventure, meriting no outside interest whatsoever. By tomorrow's standards many of today's considerable achievements will also appear equally mundane. Therefore, punch-drunk from all the recent advances (many detailed in this book), I will make no predictions concerning the years ahead, with prediction about the future, as Bohr pointed out, being so very difficult.

The only certainty, from my personal point of view, is that I will continue to enjoy ballooning, watching the world go by, savouring the sights, and wondering how and when the landing will occur at yet another unknown destination. Once I was privileged to fly the great Charles Dollfus, veteran balloonist with more than 600 gas 'ascensions' to his credit. We took off from Nottingham castle on a magnificent English evening, and smelt and felt the air that kept us company.

'Ah, but how I love ballooning,' he said.

As epitaph that is more than good enough for me.

World records

With 15 size categories and five classes of balloon there are 75 records to be won. As all 75 are duplicated for women the total number of possibilities rises to 150. There are also four sub-classes of airships (dirigibles), with each of these further divided into 10 size categories. Once again women can win women-only records, and in consequence the number of records achievable by individuals (especially if female) is very considerable.

Within Britain the principal person keeping abreast of all this activity is Norman Pritchard. He publishes a 40-page booklet every few years which, almost immediately, has to be supplemented by a computer print-out recording relevant changes as and when someone flies higher, travels further, or stays airborne longer than some predecessor. Instead of attempting to compete with his excellent publication this book (and its appendix) has selected – with his permission, most gratefully received – some of its information to give a flavour of world ballooning records, of heights, distances and endurances acquired.

Altitude, Distance and Endurance achievements are hereby listed for the three principal forms of balloon – gas (AA), hot air (AX) and combination/Roziere (AM). For simplicity the lists which follow only provide information about the largest sizes of balloon. Of particular interest is the speed at which records have tumbled in recent years, with ballooning not only the fastest growing form of aviation but also (surely) the most competitive.

For example, the official distances achieved by hot air balloons have risen from 20.2 miles in 1966 to 4,786 miles in 1991, a 236-fold leap in those 25 years. Who could possibly have foreseen such advance back in those distant days when Lyndon Johnson was president of the United States, Harold Wilson was prime minister of Great Britain, Leonid Brezhnev ruled the Soviet Union, and the Beatles were still together?

World Altitude General

Gas balloons   AA-10 to AA-15

Date	Height	Pilot(s)
9 May 1927	28,509 ft (8,690m)	Hawthorne Gray
27 May 1931	51,793 ft (15,791m)	Auguste Piccard, Paul Kipfer
18 Aug 1932	54,789 ft (16,704m)	Auguste Piccard, Max Cosyns
30 Sept 1933	60,726 ft (18,514m)	G. Prokopiev, E. Birnbaum
11 Nov 1935	72,395 ft (22,066m)	Orvill Anderson, Albert Stevens
19 Aug 1957	101,516 ft (30,942m)	David Simons
4 May 1961	113,740 ft (34,668m)	M. D. Ross, V. A. Prather

Hot air balloons   AX-14 to AX-15

Date	Height	Pilot(s)
3 Sept 1965	9,768 ft (2,978m)	Brenda Bogan
5 Oct 1965	15,691 ft (4,783m)	Donald Piccard
10 July 1966	18,979 ft (5,785m)	William Berry
25 Aug 1966	28,585 ft (8,712m)	Tracy Barnes
9 June 1971	31,189 ft (9,506m)	Karl Stefan
12 June 1971	32,949 ft (10,043m)	Chauncey Dunn
14 July 1972	35,971 ft (10,967m)	Julian Nott
25 Jan 1974	45,836 ft (13,974m)	Julian Nott, Felix Pole
1 Aug 1979	53,185 ft (16,215m)	Chauncey Dunn
31 Oct 1980	55,134 ft (16,805m)	Julian Nott
6 June 1988	64,997 ft (19,811m)	Per Lindstrand

Roziere balloons   AM-11 to AM-15

Date	Height	Pilot(s)
18 Aug 1984	11,066 ft (3,373m)	Nick Saum
26 Aug 1985	14,574 ft (4,442m)	Henk Brink
3 Oct 1990	16,495 ft (5,029m)	Donald Cameron, Gennadi Oparin

22 Sept 1992	18,378 ft (5,603m)	Troy Bradley, Richard Abruzzo
25 Nov 1996	35,090 ft (10,695m)	Per Lindstrand

World Distance General

Gas balloons   AA-14 to AA-15

Date	Distance	Pilot(s)
10 Feb 1914	1,907.9 miles (3,052.7k)	H Berliner
25 Oct 1950	1,987.6m (3,200k)	S Sinoveev, S Gaigerov, M Kirpichev
10 Oct 1976	2,474m (3,983.2k)	Edward Yost
12 Sept 1977	2,950m (4,749.5k)	Ben Abruzzo, Maxie Anderson
17 Aug 1978	3,106.3m (5,001.2k)	Ben Abruzzo, Maxie Anderson, Larry Newman
12 Nov 1981	5,208.7m (8,382.5k)	Ben Abruzzo, Larry Newman, Rocky Aoki, Ron Clark

Hot air balloons   AX-15

Date	Distance	Pilot(s)
11 Oct 1966	20.2m (32.6k)	Deke Sonnichsen
24 Nov 1969	26.4m (42.5k)	Ray Munro
1 Feb 1970	158.4m (254.8k)	Ray Munro
31 Oct 1970	160.4m (258k)	Kurt Runzi
29 Mar 1972	196.7m (316.6k)	Matt Wiederkehr
25 Oct 1973	305.6m (542.7k)	Malcolm Forbes
7 Mar 1974	339.3m (542.7k)	Matt Wiederkehr
25 Jan 1978	350.6m (564.5k)	Phil Clark
2 Mar 1980	385.9m (621k)	Ed Chapman
30 Sept 1980	419.1m (674.5k)	Geoff Green
3 Dec 1980	493m (793.7k)	Bruce Comstock, Jeff VanAlstine

6 Mar 1981	*707.8m (1,139.2k)*	Kristian Anderson,
26 Nov 1981	*717.2m (1,154.7k)*	Helene Dorigny,
		Michel Arnould
29 Feb 1983	*745.3m (1,200k)*	Helene Dorigny,
		Michel Arnould
27 Jan 1985	*907.3m (1,460.7k)*	Harold Warner,
		Phillip Johnson
3 July 1987	*2,787.9m (4,486.5k)*	Per Lindstrand,
		Richard Branson
17 Jan 1991	*4,786.1m (7,671.9k)*	Per Lindstrand,
		Richard Branson

Roziere balloons   AM-11 to AM-15

Date	Distance	Pilot(s)
30 July 1978	*2,074.8m (3,339.1k)*	Donald Cameron,
		Christopher Davey
2 Sept 1986	*2,521.5m (4,057.7k)*	Henk Brink,
		Evilien Brink,
		Willem Hageman
14 Feb 1992	*3,163.4m (5093k)*	Thomas Feliu,
		Jesus Gonzales Green
22 Sept 1992	*3,311.4m (5,331.4k)*	Troy Bradley,
		Richard Abruzzo
22 Feb 1995	*5,437m (8,748.8k)*	Stephen Fossett
20 Jan 1997	*10,361m (16,670k)*	Stephen Fossett

World Endurance General

Gas balloons   AA-11 to AA-15

Date	Time	Pilot(s)
17 Dec 1913	*87 hours*	H Kaulen
10 Oct 1976	*107 hrs, 37 mins*	Edward Yost
17 Aug 1978	*137 hrs, 5 mins*	Ben Abruzzo,
		Maxie Anderson,
		Larry Newman

Hot air balloons   AX-15

Date	Time	Pilot(s)
5 Oct l966	*1 hr, 55 mins*	Deke Sonnichsen
1 Feb 1970	*4 hrs, 52 mins*	Ray Munro
31 Oct 1970	*6 hrs, 30 mins*	Kurt Runzi
29 Mar 1972	*8 hrs, 48 mins*	Matt Wiederkehr
14 Dec 1972	*11 hrs, 14 mins*	Bob Sparks
22 Oct 1973	*13 hrs, 5 mins*	Malcolm Forbes
7 Mar 1974	*16 hrs, 16 mins*	Matt Wiederkehr
22 Nov 1975	*18 hrs, 56 mins*	Donald Cameron,
		Chris Davey,
		Jean Costa de
		Beauregard
15 Mar 1980	*19 hrs, 12 mins*	Ed Chapman
18 June 1980	*24 hrs, 8 mins*	Bruce Comstock,
		David Schaffer
26 Nov 1981	*29 hrs, 5 mins*	Helene Dorigny,
		Michael Arnould
7 July 1984	*40 hrs, 12 mins*	Helene Dorigny,
		Michael Arnould
17 Jan 1991	*46 hrs, 15 mins*	Per Lindstrand,
		Richard Branson

Roziere balloons   AM-10 to AM-15

Date	Time	Pilot(s)
30 July 1978	*96 hrs, 24 mins*	Donald Cameron,
		Christoper Davey
14 Feb 1992	*130 hrs, 30 mins*	Thomas Feliu,
		Jesus Gonzales Green
22 Sept 1992	*144 hrs, 52 mins*	Ben Abruzzo,
		Maxie Anderson,
		Larry Newman
6 Feb 1998	*233 hrs, 55 mins*	Bertrand Piccard,
		Andy Elson,
		Wim Verstraeten

Balloon Manufacturers Around the World

Aerostar International
PO Box 5057, Sioux Falls, South Dakota 57117-5057, USA

Aerotechnik Balloons
Jiraskova 18 815 48, Bratislava, Slovakia

Avian Balloon Corporation
Building 101, 3808 N Sullivan Road, Spokane WA 99216-1607, USA

Bav Holegballons
Meszaros u. 48-54, H 1016 Budapest, Hungary

B-C Products
1017 15th Street, Greeley, Colorado 80631, USA

Boland Balloon
PO Box 51, Post Mills, Vermont 05058, USA

Cameron Balloons
St John's Street, Bedminster, Bristol BS3 4NH, UK

Cameron Balloons (US)
Newman Boulevard, Dexter, Michigan 48130, USA

Chaize Ballons
48 rue Balay, 42000 St Etienne, France

Fantasy Balloons
205 Bridge Street, New Dundee, Ontario NOB 2EO, Canada

Fire Balloons
Am Bahnhof, Schweitz (Trier), D-54338, Germany

Firefly Balloons
810 Salisbury Road, P.O.Box 827, Statesville, NC 28677, USA

Flamboyant Balloon
PO Box 149, Lanseria 1748, South Africa

Galaxy Balloons
820 Salisbury Road, Statesville, North Carolina 28677, USA

Head Balloons
PO Box 28, Helen, Georgia 30545, USA

Kavanagh Balloons
13/10 Pioneer Avenue, Thornleigh, New South Wales 2120, Australia

Kubicek
Francouzska 81, 602.00, Czech Republic

Lindstrand Balloons
Maesbury Road, Oswestry, Shropshire SY10 8ZZ, UK

National Ballooning
2004 West Euclid Avenue, Indianola, Indiana 50125, USA

Rubic
Rua Ciridao Durval 139, Vila Paulista, SP CEP 04360-020, Brazil

Sky Balloons
Redwither Tower, Wrexham Industrial Estate, Clwyd LL13 9XT, UK

Thunder & Colt
St John's Street, Bedminster, Bristol BS3 4NH, UK

Ultramagic Balloons
Aerodrom Gral. Vives Ap 171, 10-08700 Igualada, Barcelona, Spain